INTRODUCING
ISSUES WITH
OPPOSING
VIEWPOINTS®

Student Drug Testing

Lauri S. Friedman, *Book Editor*

GREENHAVEN PRESS
A part of Gale, Cengage Learning

GALE
CENGAGE Learning·

Detroit • New York • San Francisco • New Haven, Conn • Waterville, Maine • London

Elizabeth Des Chenes, *Managing Editor*

© 2012 Greenhaven Press, a part of Gale, Cengage Learning

Gale and Greenhaven Press are registered trademarks used herein under license.

For more information, contact:
Greenhaven Press
27500 Drake Rd.
Farmington Hills, MI 48331-3535
Or you can visit our Internet site at gale.cengage.com

For product information and technology assistance, contact us at

Gale Customer Support, 1-800-877-4253
For permission to use material from this text or product, submit all requests online at www.cengage.com/permissions

Further permissions questions can be e-mailed to permissionrequest@cengage.com

Articles in Greenhaven Press anthologies are often edited for length to meet page requirements. In addition, original titles of these works are changed to clearly present the main thesis and to explicitly indicate the author's opinion. Every effort is made to ensure that Greenhaven Press accurately reflects the original intent of the authors. Every effort has been made to trace the owners of copyrighted material.

Cover image © JCREATION/Shutterstock.com.

LIBRARY OF CONGRESS CATALOGING-IN-PUBLICATION DATA

Student drug testing / Lauri S. Friedman, book editor.
    p. cm. -- (Introducing issues with opposing viewpoints)
  Previous ed. edited by Patty Jo Sawvel.
  Summary: "Student Drug Testing: Should Students Be Drug Tested?; Who Should Be Drug Tested?; How Does Drug Testing Affect the School Community?"-- Provided by publisher.
  Includes bibliographical references and index.
  ISBN 978-0-7377-5686-9 (hardback : perm paper)
  1. Drug testing--United States. 2. Students--Drug use--United States. 3. Youth--Drug use--United States. I. Friedman, Lauri S.
  HV5823.5.U5S73 2011
  371.7'84--dc23
                                              2011029029

Printed in the United States of America
1 2 3 4 5 6 7 15 14 13 12 11

Contents

Chapter 3: How Does Drug Testing Affect the School Community?

Foreword

Indulging in a wide spectrum of ideas, beliefs, and perspectives is a critical cornerstone of democracy. After all, it is often debates over differences of opinion, such as whether to legalize abortion, how to treat prisoners, or when to enact the death penalty, that shape our society and drive it forward. Such diversity of thought is frequently regarded as the hallmark of a healthy and civilized culture. As the Reverend Clifford Schutjer of the First Congregational Church in Mansfield, Ohio, declared in a 2001 sermon, "Surrounding oneself with only like-minded people, restricting what we listen to or read only to what we find agreeable is irresponsible. Refusing to entertain doubts once we make up our minds is a subtle but deadly form of arrogance." With this advice in mind, Introducing Issues with Opposing Viewpoints books aim to open readers' minds to the critically divergent views that comprise our world's most important debates.

Introducing Issues with Opposing Viewpoints simplifies for students the enormous and often overwhelming mass of material now available via print and electronic media. Collected in every volume is an array of opinions that captures the essence of a particular controversy or topic. Introducing Issues with Opposing Viewpoints books embody the spirit of nineteenth-century journalist Charles A. Dana's axiom: "Fight for your opinions, but do not believe that they contain the whole truth, or the only truth." Absorbing such contrasting opinions teaches students to analyze the strength of an argument and compare it to its opposition. From this process readers can inform and strengthen their own opinions, or be exposed to new information that will change their minds. Introducing Issues with Opposing Viewpoints is a mosaic of different voices. The authors are statesmen, pundits, academics, journalists, corporations, and ordinary people who have felt compelled to share their experiences and ideas in a public forum. Their words have been collected from newspapers, journals, books, speeches, interviews, and the Internet, the fastest growing body of opinionated material in the world.

Introducing Issues with Opposing Viewpoints shares many of the well-known features of its critically acclaimed parent series, Opposing Viewpoints. The articles are presented in a pro/con format, allowing readers to absorb divergent perspectives side by side. Active reading questions preface each viewpoint, requiring the student to approach the material thoughtfully and carefully. Useful charts, graphs, and cartoons supplement each article. A thorough introduction provides readers with crucial background on an issue. An annotated bibliography points the reader toward articles, books, and websites that contain additional information on the topic. An appendix of organizations to contact contains a wide variety of charities, nonprofit organizations, political groups, and private enterprises that each hold a position on the issue at hand. Finally, a comprehensive index allows readers to locate content quickly and efficiently.

Introducing Issues with Opposing Viewpoints is also significantly different from Opposing Viewpoints. As the series title implies, its presentation will help introduce students to the concept of opposing viewpoints and learn to use this material to aid in critical writing and debate. The series' four-color, accessible format makes the books attractive and inviting to readers of all levels. In addition, each viewpoint has been carefully edited to maximize a reader's understanding of the content. Short but thorough viewpoints capture the essence of an argument. A substantial, thought-provoking essay question placed at the end of each viewpoint asks the student to further investigate the issues raised in the viewpoint, compare and contrast two authors' arguments, or consider how one might go about forming an opinion on the topic at hand. Each viewpoint contains sidebars that include at-a-glance information and handy statistics. A Facts About section located in the back of the book further supplies students with relevant facts and figures.

Following in the tradition of the Opposing Viewpoints series, Greenhaven Press continues to provide readers with invaluable exposure to the controversial issues that shape our world. As John Stuart Mill once wrote: "The only way in which a human being can make some approach to knowing the whole of a subject is by hearing what can be said about it by persons of every variety of opinion and studying all modes in which it can be looked at by every character of mind. No wise man ever acquired his wisdom in any mode but this." It is to this principle that Introducing Issues with Opposing Viewpoints books are dedicated.

Introduction

Since schools first began testing sectors of the student body for drug use, teachers, parents, administrators, and students have argued for and against the practice, using a variety of arguments. Classic debates include whether testing reduces or increases student drug use, whether it discourages students from participating in extracurricular activities, and whether it is an illegal or inappropriate invasion of privacy. But the economic recession that began in 2008 has offered educational stakeholders a new framework for discussing this issue: its price. Indeed, as states have slashed school budgets and pushed the costs of extracurricular activities and classroom materials onto families and communities, student drug testing has been cast increasingly as an issue of finances. In short, with drastic cuts to school budgets, schools may not be able to afford drug testing.

Some argue that student drug testing is affordable and even cheap, considering the benefits it provides. According to the Drug Free America Foundation, Inc., drug tests cost only $10 to $30 per student, "a cost that is nominal compared to its true worth."[1] Furthermore, schools with drug testing programs are eligible to receive federal funding that has been set aside specifically, and exclusively, for this purpose. In other words, student drug testing programs do not typically siphon resources away from any other program or department because funds have been set aside expressly for them. In fact, at least twenty-nine states have received millions of dollars from the US Department of Education's Office of Safe and Drug-Free Schools (OSDFS) to develop or expand student drug testing programs. This money has been made available so schools do not have to choose between drug testing and other programs.

But no matter the cost, proponents of student drug testing argue that the money is well spent and for a critical cause: the saving of young lives. One person who believes this is Donald Hooton, who in 2003 lost his son Taylor because of the boy's steroid abuse. "If the cost of the program can prevent our student athletes from heading down the path that caused my son to take his life, I believe their family, friends and team would agree it is worth it," says Hooton.[2] Indeed, if thousands of dollars are spent and just one student is saved from death or devastation, Hooton and others think it is more than worth it.

Opponents of student drug testing programs disagree, however, and challenge the claim that such programs cost but a few dollars per student. Drug tests may be as cheap as $10 or $20 individually, but when a test needs to be purchased for each student in a school or district, total costs mount quickly. Also adding to costs are lab fees, test administrator fees, and the salaries of in-school drug counselors. In Texas, for example, a sixteen-month drug testing program tested more than forty-five thousand students, at a cost of nearly $3 million.

Furthermore, one can analyze the issue from the perspective of how much a single positive test costs. Student drug testing programs tend to yield very few positive test results; opponents say that this is either because students have figured out how to beat the tests or because drug use is not really that big of a problem in most schools. Spending millions to net a few positive tests, then, makes the cost of each positive test enormous. For example, the Drug Free Alliance found that in Dublin, Ohio, it cost $3,181 to yield a single positive test (the school system spent $35,000 administering 1,473 tests, only 11 of which ended up being positive). In Texas, because only 20 positives resulted from the 45,000 tests administered, the cost of each positive test was more than $150,000.

Even more outrageous was the money spent by the University of Texas's University Interscholastic League, which in the fall of 2009 spent $2 million testing 3,133 university students. They found just 2 positives, for a cost of $1 million per positive test. "Think, at least for a second, about how else that money could have been used to improve the quality of education—purchasing new books, hiring more teachers or at least not firing some, decreasing the size of classrooms, constructing new buildings for overcrowded schools, providing more free lunches and instituting training," said Galveston County *Daily News* columnist Evan Mohl. "Yet, the state decided to spend hard-to-find money on finding two steroid users. It's a waste and in some ways highway robbery."[3] Mohl and others think drug testing programs are a really expensive way to prove that drug abuse is just not that big of a problem in most schools and universities, at least not a big enough one to warrant spending millions on it, especially in tough economic times.

Whether student drug testing is a worthwhile use of limited school resources is just one of the issues explored in *Introducing Issues with Opposing Viewpoints: Student Drug Testing.* Other classic issues—such as whether student drug testing violates privacy and what effect it has on drug use and student participation in extracurricular activities— are explored in pro/con article pairs by passionate, expert voices on the topic. Guided reading questions and essay prompts lead readers to form their own opinions on this issue.

Notes

1. Drug Free America Foundation, Inc., "Student Drug Testing Is Part of the Solution," December 5, 2008. www.dfaf.org/content /student-drug-testing-part-solution.
2. Donald Hooton, "Taylor's Law Shows Steroid Enforcement Is Working," *Dallas Morning News,* July 14, 2008.
3. Evan Mohl, "Steroid Testing Not Worth the Money," *Daily News* (Galveston County, TX), March 25, 2010. http://galvestondaily news.com/story.lasso?ewcd=a0086fff529ce737.

Chapter 1

Should Students Be Drug Tested?

A student is pictured with two swabs in his mouth that will be used to obtain samples of his mouth fluids. The samples will be tested for the presence of drugs.

Students Should Be Randomly Drug Tested

Jeff Bergosh

"Testing will provide students a buffer against strong pro-drug peer-pressure."

In the following viewpoint Jeff Bergosh argues that randomly testing students for drug use makes schools safer places. He discusses the plans of a Florida school board to randomly test its students, arguing that such a program is an appropriate response to the growing problem of drug use and drug-related school expulsions in that county. Bergosh contends that when students think they might be drug tested, it makes it easier for them to turn down drugs out of fear they will be kicked off their sports team or barred from participating in another extracurricular activity. He concludes that randomly drug testing students is a good way to keep them off drugs.

Bergosh represents District 1 on Florida's Escambia County School Board.

The Escambia County School Board [in Florida] is preparing to take a bold step forward in an effort to minimize the presence of drugs on our school campuses.

In addition to the current daily drug dog searches at randomly chosen middle and high schools, the board is preparing a student drug-testing policy. A random testing policy was discussed during a series of meetings over the last several months. Recently, a draft testing plan was developed by a committee comprised of the School Board attorney, members of School District staff, parents, community members and local business leaders.

FAST FACT

Seventy percent of respondents to a 2002 poll by CNN/*USA Today*/Gallup said they thought student drug testing should be allowed.

A Reasonable Policy

This initial draft policy, presented to the board on Dec. 9, [2010,] calls for students to submit a consent form authorizing random drug screening if they wish to drive their vehicles on school property, participate in athletics or become involved in extra-curricular programs. Not every student will be required to submit a consent form—just those who wish to participate in the named activities. This proposed policy is the latest addition to the district's evolving, comprehensive drug awareness plan, spawned following a contentious School Board workshop held in May.

While some look at the issue of drugs in schools through rose-colored glasses and proclaim the problem is "in check," the facts prove otherwise.

Random Testing Keeps Students Safe

The number of drug-related expulsions in Escambia County schools jumped from 71 in the 2008–2009 school year to 83 in 2009–2010—an increase of nearly 17 percent. A recent analysis of the Florida Youth Substance Abuse Surveys from 2007–2010 indicates an increase in adolescent use of marijuana from 15 percent in 2007 to 19 percent in 2010.

Drug abusers are a societal problem. But drugs seep over from communities and into schools, and that is why the School Board is taking action. This issue is about student safety, no matter what one's viewpoint may be on the subject of decriminalizing certain drugs. Even if it was legal, marijuana does not belong on campuses, like alcohol and abused legal prescription medicines.

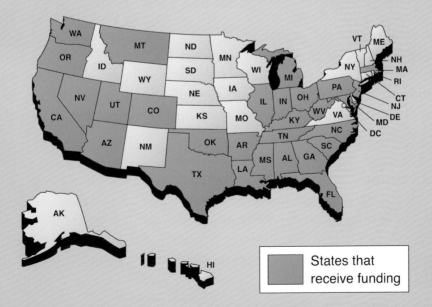

States That Receive Federal Funding for Student Drug Testing Programs

By 2008 twenty-nine states had received money from the US Department of Education's Office of Safe and Drug-Free Schools to expand student drug testing programs.

States that receive funding

Taken from: US Department of Education's Office of Safe and Drug-Free Schools and the Student Drug-Testing Institute, 2008.

According to the Florida Youth Substance Abuse Surveys, adolecent use of marijuana rose from 15 percent to 19 percent between 2007 and 2010.

Our drug awareness plan is helping our schools become safer. Testing will be a vital addition to this comprehensive approach. The School Board's thoughtfully conceived testing plan delineates the process of how the students will be randomly selected and also how any positive test results will be handled. Data will be confidential and all applicable state and federal laws will be followed. Students will receive appropriate counseling and assistance if necessary, and avenues for redemption will be available to students who make poor choices.

Random Testing Helps Students Say No

The testing component will be the strongest tool available to deter students from taking drugs. Signs and slogans are fine, but if students know they can be tested, and testing positive for drugs could preclude participation in sports or other extra-curricular activities, this will help students say NO. If students know a positive test could jeopardize a college scholarship, students will be empowered to say NO. Testing will provide students a buffer against strong pro-drug peer-pressure.

Obstreperous, discordant civil-libertarian types may oppose this plan—this is sad yet predictable. But few will be able to deny the powerful impact a random drug-screening regimen will have on student behavior and decision making; when enacted, it will reduce the amount of drugs brought to schools, making our campuses and students safer.

EVALUATING THE AUTHOR'S ARGUMENTS:

In this viewpoint Jeff Bergosh claims that students face heavy pressure from their peers to take drugs. How do you think Marsha Rosenbaum, author of the following viewpoint, would respond to this claim? Quote from both texts in your answer.

Students Should Not Be Randomly Drug Tested

Marsha Rosenbaum

"Proceed with extreme caution when it comes to student drug testing, as it may be doing more harm than good."

Not only is randomly testing students for drugs ineffective, but it may harm at-risk students, Marsha Rosenbaum argues in the following viewpoint. Rosenbaum suggests that drug testing is a poor way to detect which students actually use drugs—the tests are easy to beat, she says, and many students will fall through the cracks. Worse, drug testing students undermines the trust they feel for their parents and teachers and might encourage some students to experiment with drugs or chemicals that cannot be detected by the test. Rosenbaum concludes that there is no sure-fire way to reduce student drug use and that testing is not only inefficient but dangerous.

Rosenbaum is director of the Drug Policy Alliance, a drug education project for parents and teens. She has served as the principal investigator on studies published by the National Institute on Drug Abuse about heroin addiction, cocaine, drug use during pregnancy, and other issues.

AS YOU READ, CONSIDER THE FOLLOWING QUESTIONS:

1. What does Rosenbaum say were the findings of a National Institute on Drug Abuse study on seventy-six thousand students in schools with and without a drug testing program?
2. About how much do drug tests costs, according to the author?
3. What three signs does Rosenbaum say parents should look for if they are concerned that their child is using drugs?

The Office of National Drug Control Policy descends upon San Diego today [February 22, 2006,] to host the second of four "summits" around the country promoting random student drug testing.

With [now-former] drug czar John Walters dubbing the program a "silver bullet," enthusiastic conference presenters will no doubt sound as though they have the definitive plan for preventing teen drug use. Backed with a federal budget of more than $9 million and looking for a quick fix to a complicated problem, the push is on. As the mother of four, a National Institute on Drug Abuse scholar, and director of a drug education project for parents of teens, I urge San

In 2006 federal drug czar John Walters (pictured) promoted random drug testing in schools by declaring the Office of National Drug Control Policy program on random drug testing to be a "silver bullet" to battle drug use. The author disagrees with that policy.

Diego's educators and parents to be wary of "feel good" promises and to proceed with extreme caution when it comes to student drug testing, as it may be doing more harm than good.

Testing Does Not Reduce Drug Use

Consider the very real pitfalls: Random drug testing has not been proven to deter drug use. In 2003, the National Institute on Drug Abuse funded the largest study ever conducted on the topic. Seasoned researchers compared 76,000 students in schools with and without a drug testing program. They found no differences in illegal drug use among students from both sets of schools.

> **FAST FACT**
>
> In a 2006 policy statement, the American Academy of Pediatrics cited a national survey that found that 83 percent of physicians disagreed with drug testing in public schools.

Urine testing, the most common and inexpensive form of drug testing, is invasive and alienating. The collection of a specimen is a humiliating violation of privacy, especially embarrassing for an adolescent. Testing can, therefore, have the unanticipated effect of keeping students from participating in after-school, extracurricular programs—activities that would fill their time during the peak teenage drug-using hours from 3 p.m. to 6 p.m.

Testing Is Expensive and Breaks Trust

Random testing also can infuse an insidious sense of suspicion into the delicate student-teacher relationship, which contributes to a hostile school environment. This is particularly troubling in light of research showing the strong correlation between school connectedness and student success. Drug testing is expensive. School districts across the country, including many in Southern California, are in financial crisis. With costs ranging between $10 and $75 per test, per student, even with federal subsidies, schools simply cannot afford to spend thousands of dollars each year for a program of questionable effectiveness while valuable extracurricular programs struggle to survive. Then

Drug Testing Students Is Expensive

In 2008 forty-nine schools, districts, or boards of education in twenty states received nearly $6 million in federal aid to develop or expand student drug testing programs.

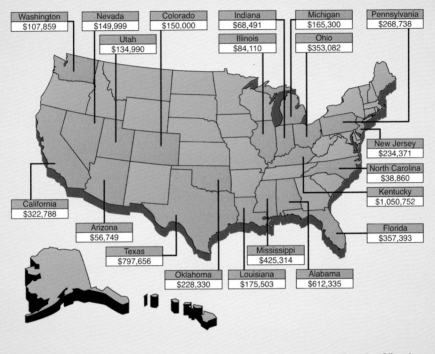

Washington	$107,859
Nevada	$149,999
Colorado	$150,000
Indiana	$68,491
Michigan	$165,300
Pennsylvania	$268,738
Utah	$134,990
Illinois	$84,110
Ohio	$353,082
New Jersey	$234,371
North Carolina	$38,860
Kentucky	$1,050,752
California	$322,788
Arizona	$56,749
Florida	$357,393
Texas	$797,656
Mississippi	$425,314
Oklahoma	$228,330
Louisiana	$175,503
Alabama	$612,335

Taken from: Congressional Notification FY 2008 Grant Award Recipients, US Department of Education, Office of Safe and Drug-Free Schools, June 4, 2008.

there are the problems associated with maintaining confidentiality and school districts' legal liability in cases, for example, of false positives or breaches of confidentiality.

Testing is inefficient when it comes to detecting drug problems. Though it may provide a false sense of security among school officials and parents, testing detects only a tiny fraction of users and misses too many who might be in trouble.

Sending Students the Wrong Message

The National Council on Alcoholism and Drug Dependence cautions that the risk of testing students for illicit drugs, "will be understood (as a) signal that alcohol and tobacco are of lesser danger." Indeed, alcohol is the overwhelming drug of choice for high school students, and the most dangerous. The vast majority of drug testing programs do not test for alcohol. Even if schools incurred the additional cost, since alcohol is undetectable in bodily fluids within a few hours, a student could easily "tie one on" on Saturday night and still test negative by Monday morning.

The notion that students need drug testing to help them say "no," is questionable. The 2005 "State of Our Nation's Youth" survey found that, contrary to popular belief, most teens are not pressured to use drugs. Instead, they are influenced by their parents, with whom 75 percent say they have a good relationship. For this reason, last year [2005] the 1-million-member California State PTA joined both the state Senate and the Assembly in opposing random, suspicionless drug testing in California schools.

"As parents, we're certainly concerned about addressing issues of student drug abuse," said spokeswoman Kathy Moffat in a July 2004 *Los Angeles Times* article, "but a random drug-testing program implies there is no trust." Random drug testing may seem a panacea, but it is fraught with social, emotional and financial problems. If we are truly intent on helping students, we should listen to drug-abuse professionals who know that detection of problems requires careful attention to signs such as truancy, erratic behavior and falling grades.

Testing Does More Harm than Good

Those in decision-making roles would be wise to listen to physicians such as Dr. Howard Taras of the UCSD [University of California–San Diego] School of Medicine, member of the American Academy of Pediatrics and chief medical consultant of the San Diego Unified School District:

"Any school currently operating a drug screening program must also have a scrupulous evaluation of the program's potential benefits and of the program's potential harms. Only results of such careful evaluations can and should guide parents and school administrators to do what's best for our youth." Before we leap into a program that uses students as guinea pigs, we should examine the many repercussions, pitfalls and alternatives to random drug testing. There simply is no "silver bullet."

Viewpoint

3

Student Drug Testing Is Effective

Wayne Laugesen

"Children must know that if they use drugs they are likely to get caught."

In the following viewpoint Wayne Laugesen argues that drugs are available everywhere and that parents and teachers cannot control the supply or protect their children and students from them. They must therefore arm them with tools to help them say no to drugs. One of these tools, says Laugesen, is drug testing. The knowledge that their drug use will be detected is enough to deter many children from ever trying them, he says. Laugesen suggests several ways in which adults can drug test the children in their life. They can either sign them up for public programs, test them at home, or have them tested by their doctor. Regardless of the method or setting, Laugesen concludes that parents and guardians have the right to keep their children off drugs and should use random drug testing to do so.

Laugesen is editorial page editor of the Colorado Springs newspaper *The Gazette*.

AS YOU READ, CONSIDER THE FOLLOWING QUESTIONS:
1. What is the ideal setting in which to drug test a child, according to Laugesen?
2. What does the phrase "chicken feed" mean in the context of the viewpoint?
3. What drug does Laugesen say is being used at Cheyenne Mountain High School?

Rational adults agree that children should not abuse drugs, yet they're torn over the issue of random drug tests for kids.

Drug laws and enforcement have failed the culture miserably, mostly serving to empower and enrich the criminal thugs who are delighted to facilitate black market drug trading. Children are their easiest targets.

Parents and teachers cannot possibly control the supply of drugs, so they must work on the demand side of the equation by discouraging drug consumption.

The cost of a drug testing kit is about forty dollars. Although each kit can be used only once, the author says, the cost is inexpensive compared with the cost of rehabilitating a child who becomes addicted to drugs.

Information and love are the best anti-drug available. Children who receive daily anti-drug messages from people who love them are at a tremendous advantage against the cunning drug dealer or drug-abusing classmate.

But information and love aren't always enough. Children must also know that parents and others in positions of trust are not leaving fate entirely to trust. Children must know that if they use drugs they are likely to get caught.

What's the best way to tell them they will get caught? To administer occasional random drug tests. Ideally, random drug tests of teens and pre-teens are conducted at home by parents and guardians. Another great option is for parents or guardians to request drug tests while taking children to physicians for checkups or athletic physicals.

Drug tests aren't free. Tests that screen for most substances cost about $40 at pharmacies and each can be used once. But the price is chicken feed relative to the cost of trying to save a child who develops a drug addiction.

Cheyenne Mountain School District 12 has embarked upon a program to provide random drug tests for high school students whose parents volunteer them. Enrollment in the program is $30 for each student, and it doesn't guarantee a random test. Students who fail drug tests will face disciplinary actions, including dismissal from extra-curricular activities and loss of on-campus driving privileges.

The D-12 program provides an acceptable option for parents and guardians who decline to manage this responsibility themselves. But anyone enrolling a child in the program should realize they may be giving public employees—people not part of the family—access to information that could someday harm a child. No matter what anyone promises, you cannot be guaranteed that a hot urinary analysis conducted by a school will not become public knowledge. The pun-

FAST FACT

In 1998 and 2002, the US Court of Appeals ruled in two separate cases (*Todd et al. v. Rush County Schools* and *Joy v. Penn-Harris-Madison School Corp.*) that student drug testing is legal when students have parking passes for school property or when they are driving on school property.

How Many American Schools Test Students for Drugs?

Because the United States Department of Education has not required school districts to report information about random student drug testing programs, exact official numbers on programs are unknown. Using data from multiple sources, the Drug-Free Projects Coalition estimates that at least 16.5 percent of all US public school districts have random drug testing programs and at least 1 percent of districts add testing programs each year.

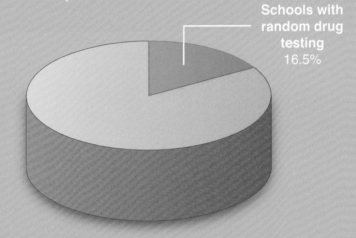

Schools with random drug testing
16.5%

Taken from: C.E. Edwards, "How Many Public School Districts Currently Test Students for Illicit Drugs on a Random Basis?," Drug-Free Projects Coalition, June 2008.

ishment itself could provide grist for the rumor mill or some other child's Facebook page.

It's great that D-12 is offering drug screenings, especially in the wake of discovering a heroin problem at Cheyenne Mountain High School that district officials described as "significant."

Before signing up, however, consider the alternative of a home-based drug-testing regimen—one that guarantees an occasional random test. Or consider requesting drug tests at each child's next visit to the doctor, where patient-confidentiality laws will keep it all in the family.

Parents and guardians have the option to keep their children off drugs. Random drug testing of children plays an important role in exercising that option.

EVALUATING THE AUTHOR'S ARGUMENTS:

In the viewpoint you just read, Wayne Laugesen uses facts, examples, and reasoning to make his argument that students should be drug tested. He does not, however, use any quotations to support his point of view. If you were to rewrite this article and insert quotations, what authorities might you quote? Where would you place quotations, and why?

Viewpoint

4

Student Drug Testing Can Have Unintended Consequences

Brendan Benedict

> "*Student drug testing programs actually may lead adolescents to engage in more risky behaviors, such as Friday-night binge drinking, which will not show up on a drug test.*"

In addition to not reducing student drug abuse, Brendan Benedict argues in the following viewpoint, drug testing is counterproductive: Students who test positive are suspended from extracurricular activities or from school entirely, which only gives them more free time to use drugs. Such tests also violate student privacy, he claims. Although the results of tests claim to be kept confidential, in his opinion it would be common knowledge among the student body who is suspended from school, and why. A student's confidential information could be further compromised in the event they received a false positive and had to reveal if they were on a certain medication. Above all, Benedict says, fear is not a deterrent for drug use. He concludes the best way to keep students off drugs is to make school a place where students feel safe, trusted, and trustworthy.

Benedict is cofounder of the group Students Morally Against Random Testing (SMART).

AS YOU READ, CONSIDER THE FOLLOWING QUESTIONS:
1. According to Benedict, what is the American Academy of Pediatrics' position on drug testing programs, and why?
2. What inhalants does Benedict say students might experiment with as the result of drug tests?
3. Who is Chris Steffner and how does she factor into the author's argument?

As a senior at Allentown High School, I served as vice president of Life-Savers, a club dedicated to preventing student substance abuse. This year our Board of Education proposed a policy that would require students who wish to participate in extracurricular activities to submit to random urinalysis tests for illicit drug use. While I understand the desire to do more, I believe the policy will do more harm than good. My fellow students and I are organizing against this policy, which is ineffective, discounts student input, invades privacy and erodes trust.

In response to the proposal, I joined with my peers to form a group, Students Morally Against Random Testing (SMART), to mobilize opposition to student drug testing. Composed of more than 250 students, parents and alumni, we are an active voice at board meetings. We have asked the board to reject the drug testing proposal and submitted a petition with at least 450 signatures from high school students.

> **FAST FACT**
>
> In 1985, New Jersey's supreme court ruled in the case *Odenheim v. Carlstadt-East Rutherford Regional School District* that drug testing is illegal, citing that the number of students who tested positive for drugs (28 for marijuana) compared to the size of the student population (520) did not justify using urinalysis.

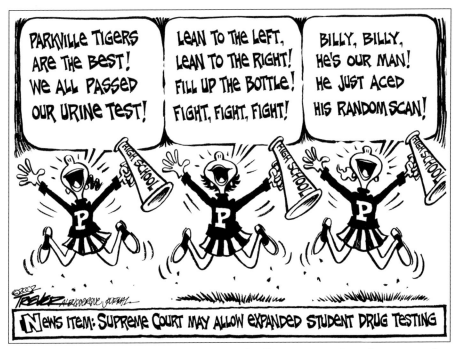

We presented the board with scientific research that found drug testing to be ineffective in reducing student drug use. A pair of University of Michigan studies, conducted in 2003, compared students in schools with and without a drug testing program and found virtually no difference in illegal drug use. Additionally, the American Academy of Pediatrics points to research indicating that student drug testing programs actually may lead adolescents to engage in more risky behaviors, such as Friday-night binge drinking, which will not show up on a drug test Monday morning.

The program can be counterproductive, as students who test positive are suspended from extracurricular activities, giving them more unsupervised time during the peak hours of student drug use. It might also prompt students to move to inhalants such as Freon or household cleaners, which are equally dangerous and will not show up on the screening.

The board should take seriously the privacy concerns of students. While the administration makes promises about confidentiality, students who are suspended from activities would be the target of

A lab technician performs a urinalysis test for drugs. The author contends that, along with other harmful effects, testing students for drug use leads to a breakdown in trust between school officials and students.

rumors and gossip, a pervasive force at our school. To protect against false positives, the school requires parents and students to disclose prescriptions and medical information, raising anxiety about this information getting out. Privacy issues are not something to be dismissed lightly.

Fear is a final byproduct of the policy. Proponents label this a "deterrent," but in actuality it breaks down trust between administrators and students. The board seems ready for a program that embraces a mentality of "guilty until proven innocent," with every student a suspect. Creating an environment of trust, where students feel connected to school, is the most effective way to keep students out of trouble with drug use.

Chris Steffner, principal of Hackettstown High School, gave a presentation in favor of testing at a recent board meeting. This is the same woman who said, "Fear in the mind of a teenager is a wonderful thing." Not only is this statement blatantly offensive to any teenager, but it is seriously misguided. No student deserves to live in fear. Growing up afraid is not conducive to education.

Students across New Jersey will continue to fight against wasteful and ineffective random student drug testing. The Upper Freehold Regional school board is scheduled to vote on the policy on June 18. New Jersey educators should listen to the science, the experts and their students and "just say no" to random drug testing.

EVALUATING THE AUTHOR'S ARGUMENTS:

Brendan Benedict cofounded the group Students Morally Against Random Testing (SMART) when he was a senior in high school. Think about the issue of drug testing at your school. Are students ever drug tested? If so, are there any student organizations that favor or oppose the program? If not, has a student drug testing program ever been suggested? Investigate the history of drug testing at your school by interviewing students, teachers, and administrators. Write two to three paragraphs on what you discover.

Student Drug Testing Violates Privacy

"We do not allow police to randomly stop people on the streets to see if they have drugs, and the school district should follow the same code of conduct."

Examiner.com

The following viewpoint was published by the Allentown, Millstone, Roosevelt, and Upper Freehold, New Jersey, edition of Examiner.com, a website that generates local news and content in more than sixty cities and towns in the United States. The authors argue that random drug testing violates student privacy. Substance abuse is not a large enough problem in schools to warrant widespread, random drug testing, contend the authors. Furthermore, the authors argue that students have the right to privacy and the right to be free from unreasonable searches, and they suggest that Supreme Court decisions that have found that drug tests do not violate these rights are unfair and wrong. Random drug testing unfairly targets students without cause, the authors conclude, and therefore the practice is a violation of privacy.

Anyone interested in protecting their children's rights should attend the June 18 [2008] Upper Freehold [New Jersey] Regional Board of Education meeting where the merits of a random drug testing policy for high school students in extracurricular activities will be discussed and voted on.

The school district is following the lead of two questionable U.S. Supreme Court rulings in 1995 and 2002 that found drug testing does not violate a student's Fourth Amendment rights to privacy and freedom from unreasonable searches because schools have a responsibility to protect the health and well-being of the student population. These rulings are flimsy, arguing that students in extracurricular activities have less of a legitimate privacy interest because "school sports are not for the bashful" and "there is an element of communal undress inherent" in athletic and other extracurricular activities. Civil libertarians continue to challenge these positions, which is the first reason we implore residents to weigh in on whether the school district should enter this gray area.

Furthermore, school districts that implement random drug testing have to meet certain criteria set forth in those rulings, and we're not totally convinced the local district has. Districts have to present an immediate, legitimate concern in preventing drug use among its students and evidence of a drug problem.

More Harm than Good

According to the Upper Freehold Regional School District's annual report on violence, vandalism and substance abuse incidents, there were eight incidents involving substance abuse in the schools last year [2007–2008], which is 11 less than in 2005–06. The report notes

The student pictured here makes his feelings about drug use clear. The author discusses a school district in New Jersey in which drug use is actually on the decline.

that 22 students had been sent for drug screenings in 2006–07, 10 of whom tested positive. The previous year's report stated that seven students had been screened, with four testing positive, and in 2004–05, 37 students were screened and eight tested positive. There are about 1,151 [students] in grades 9–12.

School officials argue that random drug testing will deter drug use, but there are just as many studies that say it does as there are those that say it does not. Even the Committee on Substance Abuse and the Council on School Health of the American Academy of Pediatrics in 2007 called for more rigorous scientific evaluation to determine if such testing is effective in curbing drug use and to evaluate possible harm.

Drug Tests Violate the Law

The harm in random drug testing is that it can indirectly encourage students to use more alcohol and drugs when athletic seasons or extracurricular activities end and to use more dangerous and harmful drugs that can be excreted from the body faster than cannabis [marijuana]. Students can also resort to using harmful methods of trying to flush out their bodies to cheat a urine test.

We also encourage the school district to consider that most "random testing" procedures are open to legal challenge because it often cannot be proved that a testing subject was not targeted. There's also the question of whether or not such a policy violates the nation's Health Insurance Portability and Accountability Act (HIPAA) standards for which even the White House had no answer.

> **FAST FACT**
>
> In the 2008 case *York v. Wahkiakum*, the state of Washington banned random student drug testing after its supreme court ruled that such testing violates privacy rights as outlined in the state constitution.

Random Tests Violate Civil Liberties

We believe the school district should help protect the well-being of students by strictly enforcing its for-cause drug policy, which is already in place and allows for the testing of students who are visually intoxicated or suspected of using. The [school district] should also focus the funding it would use for random testing as well as its grant-obtaining and fundraising efforts toward more extracurricular activities and additional resources for kids who may be in trouble.

Types of Student Drug Tests

Schools can choose from three types of drug tests, each with advantages and disadvantages.

Type of Test	Pros	Cons	Window of Detection
Hair	• Donor friendly; easy to collect • Adulteration is more difficult • Can detect 6 different drugs • Test is dependable and accurate	• A lab must run and generate results • Longer time to get results • May not detect very recent drug use • Most expensive drug testing method	• Up to 90 days
Saliva	• Donor friendly; noninvasive and easy to collect the specimen • No need for a bathroom to administer the tests; can obtain samples in any environment • Can detect very recent drug use • Hard to adulterate • Can test up to 5 or 6 drugs at a time	• Short detection time period • Some smoked drugs might cause contamination of saliva and inconclusive results	• 1–3 days depending on substance and other factors
Urine	• Has a scientific and legal base for accuracy • Most flexible for testing different drugs • Cost is lower than other drug testing kits • Results can be obtained quickly • Can detect from 5 to 12 different drugs	• Need a bathroom to conduct the tests • Can be viewed as invasive or embarrassing • Limited time for detection	• 1–30 days depending on substance and other factors

Taken from: Student Drug-Testing Institute, "Developing, Implementing, and Sustaining a Student Drug-Testing Program," August 5, 2009, p. 15.

Help parents become better informed, continually review and update drug assistance counseling at the high school level, help teachers and staff better identify problem behaviors for early intervention, refer troubled students to health care professionals, and strengthen the partnership with the community's two existing drug alliances. The board could also try implementing a voluntary drug testing program to truly gauge the community's interest.

The board should also consider that expending district funds for random drug testing would reduce those for other more effective deterrents, not to mention other school programs, staff and books, which the school district already has problems funding adequately.

Even though we know there is a drug and alcohol problem in our society, we do not allow police to randomly stop people on the streets to see if they have drugs, and the school district should follow the same code of conduct. Yes, it's a shame that so many youths die from alcohol and drug-related accidents each year, but the school district should not have the sole responsibility of trying to save them, especially at the expense of civil liberties.

EVALUATING THE AUTHOR'S ARGUMENTS:

The authors of this viewpoint disagree with Supreme Court decisions that found drug testing not to violate a student's Fourth Amendment rights to privacy and freedom from unreasonable searches. Research the *Vernonia School District v. Acton* (1995) and *Board of Education of Independent School District of Pottawatomie County v. Earls* (2002), Supreme Court rulings that deal with student drug testing and write one paragraph that summarizes each case. Then, state your opinion on the matter. Do you agree that random drug testing violates a student's rights? Support your answer with evidence from the texts you have read.

Frequently Asked Questions About Student Drug Testing

Student Drug-Testing Institute

"The [US Supreme] Court upheld the constitutionality of a policy requiring student athletes to submit to random drug testing."

The Student Drug-Testing Institute (SDTI) was established by the US Department of Education's Office of Safe and Drug-Free Schools (OSDFS) in August 2008. It is tasked with providing accurate information on student drug testing (SDT) programs, including how to develop an SDT program. In the following viewpoint, SDTI argues that student drug testing does not violate student privacy. It explains that test results are kept confidential and shared only with school officials and parents. Testing programs operate in accordance with federal law that protects student privacy, also. Furthermore, SDTI points out that the US Supreme Court has upheld the constitutionality of student drug tests in two major cases. For all of these reasons, it rejects claims that student drug testing programs violate privacy and argues that such programs effectively keep students off drugs.

1. What are the long-term consequences of drug abuse for teenagers, according to the author?
2. What is *Vernonia School District v. Acton* and how does it factor into SDTI's argument?
3. What is the Family Education Rights and Privacy Act (FERPA) and how does it factor into the author's argument?

The Need for Student Drug Testing

Random student drug testing is foremost a prevention program. Drug testing is one of several tools that schools can use as part of a comprehensive drug prevention effort. Administrators, faculty, and students at schools that conduct testing view random testing as a deterrent, and it gives students a reason to resist peer pressure to try or use drugs. Drug testing can identify students who have started using drugs so that interventions can occur early, or identify students who already have drug problems, so they can be referred for assessment, counseling, or treatment. Drug abuse not only interferes with a student's ability to learn, but it can also disrupt the teaching environment, affecting other students as well. Each school or school district that wants to start a program needs to involve the entire community in determining whether student drug testing is right for their specific situation.

Although drug use among America's youth has declined in recent years, many young people continue to abuse harmful substances. The 2008 Monitoring the Future Survey shows that drug use among school-age youth has been in a state of decline since the 1990's; however, the proportions of 8th- and 12th-grade students indicating any use of an illicit drug in the 12 months prior to the survey showed rather modest increases since the previous year. Nearly half of 12th graders said that they have used drugs in their lifetime, and almost one third said that they use marijuana at least monthly. According to another survey conducted in 2006, an estimated 20.4 million Americans aged 12 or older (8.3 percent of the population) were current illicit drug users, using within the past month.

Like use of other illicit drugs, steroid usage has seen a decline since usage peaked among male teens in 1999. However, steroid abuse is still a problem for many young people. The 2008 Monitoring the Future data show that 1.2 percent of 8th graders, 1.4 percent of 10th graders, and 2.5 percent of 12th graders reported using steroids at least once in their lifetime. A survey sponsored by the Centers for Disease Control and Prevention (CDC) reported that 3.9 percent of all high school students surveyed in 2007 reported use of steroid pills/shots without a doctor's prescription at some point in their lives. This figure includes 4.8 percent of 9th graders, 3.7 percent of 10th graders, 3.1 percent of 11th graders, and 3.8 percent of 12th graders.

Prescription drug abuse is also high and is increasing. The 2008 Monitoring the Future data indicate that 15.4 percent of 12th graders reported using a prescription drug nonmedically within the past year. Vicodin, an opiate pain reliever, continues to be abused at unacceptably high levels. Many of the drugs used by 12th graders are prescription drugs or, in the case of cough medicine, are available over the counter.

Testing Programs Help Students Say No

Despite some declines in drug use, much remains to be done. Youth still face a barrage of media messages and peer pressure that promote drug use. Random student drug-testing programs are effective prevention strategies to help adolescents refuse drugs, when offered. . . .

Drug use can turn into abuse and then into addiction, trapping users in a vicious cycle that can ruin lives and destroy families. Studies have shown drug testing to be an effective tool in preventing student drug use. The expectation that they may be randomly tested is enough to make some students stop using drugs—or never start in the first place. School-based drug testing is also an excellent tool for getting students who use drugs the help they need.

According to the 2007 National Survey on Drug Use and Health students who use drugs are statistically more likely to drop out of school, bring guns to school, steal, and be involved in fighting or other delinquent behavior. Drug abuse not only interferes with a student's ability to learn, it also disrupts the orderly environment necessary for all students to succeed. Obviously, reducing the likelihood of these disruptive behaviors benefits everyone involved in a school environment.

Teens Are Particularly Vulnerable

Teens are especially vulnerable to drug abuse when the brain and body are still developing. Most teens do not use drugs, but for those that do, it can lead to a wide range of adverse effects on the brain, the body, behavior, and health.

Short term: Even a single use of an intoxicating drug can affect a person's judgment and decision-making—resulting in accidents, poor performance in a school or sports activity, unplanned risky behavior, and the risk of overdosing.

Long term: Repeated drug abuse can lead to serious problems, such as poor academic outcomes, mood changes (depending on the drug: depression, anxiety, paranoia, psychosis), and social or family problems caused or worsened by drugs. Repeated drug use can also lead to the disease of addiction. Studies show that the earlier a teen begins using drugs, the more likely he or she will develop a substance abuse problem or addiction. Conversely, if teens stay away from drugs while in high school, they are less likely to develop a substance abuse problem later in life. . . .

Drug Testing Programs Are Constitutional

The Supreme Court of the United States first determined that drug testing of student athletes is constitutional in a June 1995 decision. Voting 6 to 3 in *Vernonia School District v. Acton* the court upheld the constitutionality of a policy requiring student athletes to submit to random drug testing.

In June 2002, the U.S. Supreme Court broadened the authority of public schools to test students for illegal drugs. Voting 5 to 4 in *Pottawatomie County v. Earls,* the court ruled to allow random drug

Tecumseh Public Schools had been named in the Pottawatomie County v. Earls *lawsuit. Here, school superintendent Danny Jacobs reads congratulatory messages following the US Supreme Court's decision, which stated that the necessity of schools to rid their campuses of drugs outweighs students' right to privacy.*

tests for all middle and high school students participating in competitive extracurricular activities. The ruling greatly expanded the scope of school drug testing. . . .

Drug Testing Is Private and Confidential

This concern usually stems from a misunderstanding of the purpose of student drug testing. Foremost, the U.S. Supreme Court has ruled that student drug testing is permissible, but must be done confidentially. Schools have a responsibility to respect students' privacy, so it is vital that only the people who need to know the test results see them—parents, the student, and a school administrator, for example. The results should not be shared with anyone else, not even teachers. The purpose is not to expose and punish children for drug use, but to deter use, intervene early with those who have just begun to use, and to provide help to those who have become dependent.

Student drug-testing records should also be kept strictly confidential in accordance with the Family Education Rights and Privacy Act (FERPA), a federal law that protects the privacy of student education records. The law applies to all schools that receive funds under an applicable program of the U.S. Department of Education. Student drug-testing activities are often also covered under the Protection of Pupil Rights Amendment (PPRA). . . .

Testing Methods Are Accurate and Respect Privacy

There are several testing methods available for different types of specimens, including urine, hair, oral fluids, and sweat (patch). These methods vary in cost, reliability, drugs detected, and detection period. Schools should determine their needs and choose the method that best suits their requirements, as long as the testing procedures are conducted by a reliable source, such as a certified or nationally accredited drug-testing company or a hospital.

Various testing methods normally test for a "panel" of drugs. Typically, a drug panel tests for marijuana, cocaine, opioids, amphetamines, and PCP. If a school or community has a particular problem with other drugs, such as tobacco, ecstasy (MDMA), gamma hydroxybutyrate (GHB), or steroids, they can include testing for these drugs.

Screening tests are very accurate but not 100 percent accurate. Usually samples are divided so if an initial test is positive, a confirmation test can be conducted.

Many drug-using students are aware of techniques that supposedly detoxify their systems or mask their drug use. Popular magazines and Internet sites give advice on how to dilute urine samples, and there are even companies that sell drug-free "clean" urine or products designed to distort test results. A number of techniques

The Legality of Student Drug Testing

The US Supreme Court has twice ruled that drug testing certain students does not violate the Fourth Amendment, which protects citizens from unreasonable searches and seizures.

Place	Year	Case	Impact
Oregon	1995	*Vernonia School District 47J v. Acton*	The Court ruled that schools could randomly drug test student athletes and prohibit students who refused to submit to a test from participating. It justified its ruling by saying that because athletes change in communal dressing rooms and submit to preseason physicals, they have a lower expectation of privacy than other students. The Court also labeled athletes as school leaders who are in a position to encourage nonathletes to say no to drugs. Finally, the Court reasoned that out of all the students at a school, athletes were among the most important to subject to drug tests because they are more at risk of being immediately physically harmed during play, or of harming others during play.
Oklahoma	2002	*Board of Education of Pottawatomie County v. Earls*	The Court expanded the constitutionality of mandatory student drug testing programs by making it legal for schools to drug test all students who participate in any extracurricular activity, not just sports.

[Compiled by editor.]

and products are focused on urine tests for marijuana, but masking products increasingly are becoming available for tests of hair, oral fluids, and multiple drugs.

Most of these products do not work, are very costly, can be identified in the testing process, and must be readily available at the random time of testing. Moreover, even if the specific drug is successfully masked, the masking product itself can be detected, in which case the student using it would become an obvious candidate for additional screening and attention. In fact, some testing programs consider a test "positive" if a masking product is detected.

EVALUATING THE AUTHOR'S ARGUMENTS:

The Student Drug-Testing Institute contends that drug testing programs are designed to protect a student's privacy and that they do not violate the Constitution. How do you think each of the authors in this chapter would respond to this claim? Write one or two sentences for each author. Then, state your opinion. Do you think drug tests violate a student's privacy? Why or why not?

Chapter 2

Who Should Be Drug Tested?

Many high schools have instituted mandatory drug testing for student athletes.

Student Athletes Should Be Tested for Steroids

Donald Hooton

"Our new [testing] law is deterring high school students in the State of Texas from using anabolic steroids."

The following viewpoint was written by Donald Hooton, whose son Taylor killed himself in 2003. It is believed that Taylor's steroid use made him prone to severe depression. After his son's death, Hooton founded the Taylor Hooton Foundation, a nonprofit organization dedicated to fighting steroid use and implementing steroid testing programs in schools. Hooton argues that student athletes should be tested for steroids, because the fear of getting caught by a drug test helps student athletes say no to drugs in the same way that the fear of getting caught by the police helps drivers avoid the temptation to speed. He argues that the presence of a testing program is a deterrent to students and helps keep them off drugs. He concludes that steroids testing programs are necessary and vital for student safety.

AS YOU READ, CONSIDER THE FOLLOWING QUESTIONS:
1. How many positive tests does Hooton say resulted from more than ten thousand tests conducted by the National Center for Drug Free Sports?
2. What percentage of high school students use anabolic steroids, as reported by the author?
3. What is "steroid profiling" and why does Hooton disagree with it?

This month [July 2008] marks the tragic fifth anniversary of the suicide of my son Taylor Hooton caused by steroid-induced depression. Taylor was only seventeen. His passing has forever affected our family, but in the wake of the tragedy, I formed the Taylor Hooton Foundation to spotlight the effects of performance enhancing drugs in our children.

The Foundation's efforts led to a successful partnership with the Texas Legislature to enact Taylor's Law, which put into place the most aggressive mandatory, random steroid testing policy in the nation. The testing program established by Taylor's Law, signed into Texas state law in June 2007, is clearly working. Of the preliminary results, two positive tests resulted from over 10,000 tests conducted by the National Center for Drug Free Sports.

FAST FACT

In 2006 New Jersey became the first state to establish a statewide policy of testing high school athletes for steroids.

The primary purpose of Taylor's Law is to prevent our children from turning to steroids by providing a deterrent; the risk of getting caught gives our kids a solid reason to say no. Testing programs like this are like "speed traps" on Interstate highways. Many adults and teens drive the speed limit NOT because they know that doing such is safer and saves fuel, they do it because they know someone is watching—the fear of getting caught is greater than the desire to disobey the law. What happens when you take away the speed traps (drug tests) and everyone knows it? People start breaking the law (cheating).

Whether the program yielded two positives, 400 positives, or 1,000 positives, no one should be drawing conclusions about the extent of steroid use based on these preliminary lab results. The program was never designed to measure steroid use among high school athletes.

Kids Are Getting Help

According to the statistics from the 2007 National Youth Risk Behavior Survey, recognized as the premiere organization in this field, 3.9% of high school students in our country are abusing anabolic steroids nationally. Given that 10,407 students were tested in Texas in the past year, the results should have yielded at least 400 positive tests. Based on the preliminary results that we've read about, what we do know is:

- The random testing preliminary results of Texas students identified that 99.98% of the sampled student athletes tested clean for performance enhancing drugs.
- At least two kids are going to get help before something tragic happens.

The Olympic Analytical Laboratory at the University of California–Los Angeles, one of two in the country, is used by the National Center for Drug Free Sport to do its drug testing.

Are Drug Testing Programs Worth It?

A 2010 study found that of thousands of students tested, only a handful of positive results were found. Proponents of student drug testing programs argue that the number of positive tests is not important; it is the existence of the tests themselves that deter students from using drugs.

Substance	Number of Tests Analyzed for Each Substance	Number of Positive Tests	Percentage of Tests That Were Positive
Marijuana	3,476	23	0.7
Amphetamine or methamphetamine	3,438	5	0.1
Opiates (heroin, morphine, codeine)	3,053	0	0.0
Cocaine	3,053	0	0.0
Phencyclidine (PCP)	2,661	0	0.0
Benzodiazepine (tranquilizer)	2,334	0	0.0
Synthetic opiates	2,268	0	0.0
Barbiturate	1,942	0	0.0
Propoxyphene (pain medication)	1,942	1	0.1
Alcohol	1,662	5	0.3
Ecstasy	1,511	0	0.0
Steroids	1,424	1	0.1
Methaqualone (sedative)	1,414	0	0.0
Lysergic acid diethylamide (LSD)	1,308	0	0.0
Gamma hydroxy butyrate (GHB)	1,259	0	0.0
Nicotine	1,269	3	0.2

Taken from: US Department of Education, "The Effectiveness of Mandatory Random Student Drug Testing," July 2010.

- 10,000 kids know first-hand that we are taking this issue seriously here in Texas, and
- Millions of Texas families now know about the dangers of anabolic steroids.

Those results to me are an excellent definition of success!

Clean Competition and Healthy Athletes

When Texas student athletes compete against each other, they are often competing at the most elite levels of high school competition.

It is clear to me that our new law is deterring high school students in the State of Texas from using anabolic steroids. As a result of the rigorous consequences for failures, Texas has set itself as the standard bearer for clean sports and healthy student athletes in the nation.

I am very interested in seeing the testing results for this upcoming year when it will include football season for the first time. The Friday night lights shine brightest in our state and I am optimistic that our success in maintaining clean competition and healthy athletes will transfer to the Texas gridiron.

Continuing in the Face of Success

Some critics would like to reduce the scope of the program as a result of its initial success, while some in the press have suggested a version of "steroid profiling" stating that "state officials should focus on testing athletes who show signs of steroid abuse." If the cost of the program can prevent our student athletes from heading down the path that caused my son to take his life, I believe their family, friends and team would agree it is worth it. It's also very disheartening to think that select members of the media would so vigorously advocate profiling of any kind.

Taylor's Law was created with the intention of deterring all student-athletes from steroid abuse. So with more than 10,000 tests, our program's initial findings show that 99.98% are clean. We still have work to do. Texas must ensure that 100% of our student athletes do not fall prey to these destructive drugs. I hope Texas lawmakers will honor their charge to protect our children by continuing this successful initiative.

EVALUATING THE AUTHOR'S ARGUMENTS:

The author of this viewpoint lost his son to steroid abuse. How does knowing Donald Hooton's personal connection to this issue affect your opinion of his argument? Does it make you more inclined to agree with him? Less inclined? Explain your reasoning.

Student Athletes Should Not Be Tested for Steroids

San Angelo (TX) Standard-Times

"Nearly all of the 51,000-plus athletes who were tested not only haven't used steroids, they also never have seen them and don't know anyone who has."

In the following viewpoint, editors at Texas's *San Angelo Standard-Times* newspaper argue that there is no need to test student athletes for steroid use. They discuss a mandatory program in Texas that since 2007 has tested more than 51,000 athletes. Just a tiny fraction of these athletes have tested positive for drug use, which in the authors' opinion proves there is little need to conduct such tests. They maintain that steroid testing programs are expensive, and they lament that millions of dollars have been wasted testing for a problem that seems not to exist. The authors conclude that because there is no evidence of a steroid problem among high school athletes, school systems should end mandatory testing programs.

AS YOU READ, CONSIDER THE FOLLOWING QUESTIONS:
  1. How many of thirty-three hundred Texas athletes tested positive for steroids in spring 2010, according to the authors?
  2 How much do the editors of the *Standard-Times* say it has cost the state of Texas to yield twenty-one positive steroid tests since testing began in 2007?
  3. What do the authors say exposes students to a far greater danger than steroid use?

More evidence is in that the Texas Legislature should take a serious look at ending the state's high school steroid testing program. In July [2010], the University Interscholastic League released the results of testing done in the spring. Not one of the more than 3,300 athletes tested had a positive result. That follows fall testing, when two of 3,133 students were positive.

In 2010 Texas tested thirty-three hundred university athletes for steroid use, but none tested positive for drugs.

The results were not surprising. In fact, they closely track previous results since testing began in 2007. In those three years, more than 51,000 tests have turned up 21 positive results, at a cost of $7 million.

Some proponents say: See, it's working. Others acknowledge the tiny number of steroid users but say that even if one young person is steered away from the potential danger, the program is worth the cost.

The trouble with the first response is that there's nothing more than anecdotal evidence about how serious the problem was before 2007. It's possible—likely, even—that at the peak only a small number of athletes in a few select sports used the drugs.

Understanding Risks and Benefits

While the second argument has emotional power, it isn't entirely logical. For example, if Texas really wants to protect young people, it would prohibit them from driving, which exposes far more of them to far greater danger.

But risks are weighed against benefits, and society, through its elected officials, has judged that permitting 16-year-olds to get behind the wheel is an overall plus.

Likewise, society over time has decided that, in certain situations, basic American principles—the presumption of innocence, for example—can be sacrificed for the greater good. Thus there were few objections when the state began requiring steroid testing of high school athletes.

No Compelling Need for Testing

But before we yank a 110-pound female cross country runner from Muleshoe out of her algebra class and tell her that she can't compete unless she urinates in a cup to prove she isn't taking steroids, we owe it to her and ourselves to make certain there's a demonstrable need.

Students' Views on Steroid Use

The 2010 Monitoring the Future study found that steroid use among eighth-, tenth-, and twelfth-graders is low—less than 2 percent of students reported using steroids in the past 12 months. Students also reported that steroids are difficult to get and that most disapprove of their use. These results are evidence for some that steroid use is not a problem and, therefore, that students do not need to be tested for them.

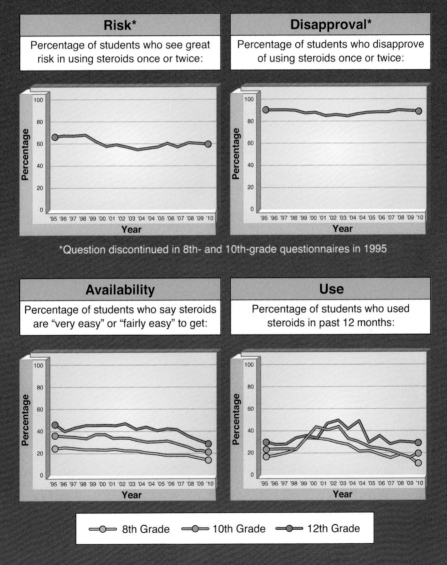

Risk*

Percentage of students who see great risk in using steroids once or twice:

Disapproval*

Percentage of students who disapprove of using steroids once or twice:

*Question discontinued in 8th- and 10th-grade questionnaires in 1995

Availability

Percentage of students who say steroids are "very easy" or "fairly easy" to get:

Use

Percentage of students who used steroids in past 12 months:

8th Grade   10th Grade   12th Grade

Taken from: Monitoring the Future/University of Michigan, "Steroids: Trends in Annual Use, Risk, Disapproval, and Availability, Grades 8, 10, 12," *National Results on Student Drug Use: Overview of Key Findings*, 2010.

We have no facts to back this up, but it seems likely that nearly all of the 51,000-plus athletes who were tested not only haven't used steroids, they also never have seen them and don't know anyone who has. This isn't a peer-pressure matter.

Testing Programs Waste Public Money

All this isn't to suggest that Texans shouldn't worry about whether young people are taking steroids. Rather, the point is that the best use of public money on this issue is to educate athletes about the dangers of steroids and to train coaches and other educators to recognize who is using them.

Partly because of the low positive results and partly because of the state's budget condition, the amount of money set aside for steroid testing has been reduced to $750,000 in this school year [2010]. That's better than $3 million, but still more than is justified.

When the next Legislature convenes in January [2011], lawmakers should make a great show about the low number of users, declare victory in the war on steroids and end the mandatory testing program.

EVALUATING THE AUTHOR'S ARGUMENTS:

In this viewpoint, the editors at the *San Angelo Standard-Times* argue that the low number of positive steroid tests show that a widespread testing program is not necessary. In the previous viewpoint Donald Hooton argues that the number of positive tests is immaterial—the point of a testing program is to deter, not measure, use. What do you think? Do low numbers of positive tests indicate a lack of need for a steroid testing program? Why or why not?

Student Athlete Steroid Testing Programs Should Profile At-Risk Athletes

Rick Cantu

"With all due respect to distance runners, there has never been a whisper about steroid abuse in the cross country world."

In the following viewpoint Rick Cantu argues that randomly testing student athletes for steroids is a waste of time and money. Instead, he says, steroid testing programs should focus on the athletes most likely to be using steroids, such as suspiciously large and fast football and baseball players. He discusses a steroid testing program in Texas that randomly tests athletes in all sports, including golf, tennis, and cross-country running. Cantu argues that it is not surprising that very few positive tests were found, since athletes in these sports tend not to use steroids. A better use of sparse resources, in his opinion, would be to focus on testing the athletes who are most likely to use steroids. Cantu warns that because random testing programs do not target the right kinds of student athletes, they are at risk of being cut from budgets. He recommends doing away with random testing and honing in on the athletes that are most at risk for abusing such drugs.

Cantu is a staff reporter for the Austin, Texas, newspaper the *American Statesman.*

AS YOU READ, CONSIDER THE FOLLOWING QUESTIONS:
1. How much money did Texas allocate to its steroid testing program in 2007, according to Cantu?
2. During the 2009–2010 academic year, of 6,441 tests for steroids, how many does the author say came back positive?
3. In 2009–2010, how many soccer players does Cantu say were tested for steroids? How many basketball players and cross-country runners?

What's wrong with this picture? There are plenty of 280-pound offensive linemen in Texas high schools who have never been tested for steroids or performance-enhancing drugs, but there are rail-thin cross country runners who have lifted their arms and taken the needle.

When [Texas] Lt. Gov. David Dewhurst championed the testing program for the state's 1,300 public high schools in 2007, his intentions were pure.

The sports pages offer weekly reminders that drug-enhanced cheaters exist—from Major League Baseball and the NFL to the Tour de France and track and field—and it makes sense to deter young athletes from taking steroids in high school.

So with Dewhurst leading the charge, the largest steroid-testing program in the country was allocated $6 million to randomly select between 20,000 and 25,000 of the state's estimated 740,000 student-athletes at public schools.

But this is a program without teeth, one hamstrung by political concessions and bowing to political correctness, and while some believe random steroid testing has been an effective deterrent, others can rightly argue that it's a complete waste of money.

The University Interscholastic League [UIL], in charge of implementing the program, has reported only 21 positive results out of more than 50,000 student-athletes tested since February 2008.

Last spring [2010], not a single positive result emerged from the testing of 3,308 student-athletes.

The validity of the testing program has resurfaced this fall because of large budget cuts inflicted on the program. The flush annual budget of $6 million just three years ago has been slashed to $750,000 this year.

While some in Dewhurst's camp call testing a "win-win" situation, there have been few cheaters caught, although one could argue that some athletes are scared away from steroids because of the possibility of being tested.

David Dewhurst, lieutenant governor of Texas, was a strong proponent of the state's program that randomly tested student athletes for steroids. However, results did not justify the program's $6 million annual budget, which, after three years of testing, was cut to $750,000 per year.

Random Testing Is Ineffective

Yes, these tests hardly reveal the true number of athletes who have dabbled in performance-enhancing drugs. Maybe because of the type of athletes randomly selected for testing.

During the 2009–10 academic year, 6,441 tests for steroids were administered to UIL athletes. Only two came back with positive results.

Among those tested were 798 soccer players, 617 basketball players, 374 tennis players, 149 cross country runners, 149 golfers and 293 volleyball players.

With all due respect to distance runners, there has never been a whisper about steroid abuse in the cross country world.

Test Athletes Most Likely to Be Using

The 2,380 tests administered to athletes competing in soccer, basketball, tennis, cross country, golf and volleyball could have been used on, say, some of the beefy football players who were bypassed. Or a few more baseball power hitters or the track athletes with perfectly sculpted bodies.

But that's not how the law was adopted, and the state's football coaches would have barked if the program was aimed solely at their sport. Same for those coaches in baseball or track and field.

With so few student-athletes testing positive for steroid use, don't be surprised if the testing program is eliminated in a few years. No use spending significant money on something that ferrets out only one or two cheaters a year.

In the meantime, the skinny girl who plays JV [junior varsity] basketball has just as good a chance to be randomly selected for drug testing as the 280-pound football player we hear about every Friday night.

> **FAST FACT**
>
> According to the 2002 study "Anabolic Steroids and Pre-adolescent Athletes: Prevalence, Knowledge, and Attitudes," 64 percent of students who used steroids said they did so to increase their strength; 48 percent said to increase their size; 44 percent said to improve their physical appearance; and 17 percent said because their peers were users.

EVALUATING THE AUTHOR'S ARGUMENTS:

In this viewpoint Rick Cantu recommends doing away with random testing programs and instead honing in on the athletes most likely to be using steroids. This is a controversial practice called profiling, which is sometimes used by police to target people most likely to be criminals (rather than screening the general public). Do you think profiling football or baseball players for steroid use is unfair and inappropriate, or is it a wise use of limited resources? Explain your reasoning and quote from the texts you have read in your answer.

The Entire Student Body Should Be Drug Tested

Harry Connick, Yvonne Gelpi, and Aaron Middleberg

"The No. 1 thing that made a difference was, every single student in De La Salle had a reason to say no."

In the following viewpoint three people involved in drug testing in New Orleans schools testify to its effectiveness. The first emphasizes the program's usefulness in reducing the demand side of the drug problem, rather than being another attempt to reduce the supply side where tax dollars are usually spent. The second highlights the reduction in percentage of students testing positive between the first and last years of the drug-testing program, in which all students were tested. The last emphasizes the benefit to him of having a reason to say no to peers pressuring him to try drugs.

The Subcommittee on Criminal Justice, Drug Policy, and Human Resources was an investigations and oversight subcommittee of the House of Representatives, 106th Congress, with John L. Mica, representative from Florida, as chair. Harry Connick was District Attorney in New Orleans;

"Drug Testing in Schools: An Effective Deterrent?," Hearing before the Subcommittee on Criminal Justice, Drug Policy, and Human Resources, of the Committee on Government Reform, House of Representatives, 106th Congress, 2nd Session, May 30, 2000.

Yvonne Gelpi was principal of De La Salle High School in New Orleans; and Aaron Middleberg is a former student at De La Salle High School.

AS YOU READ, CONSIDER THE FOLLOWING QUESTIONS:
1. What is the difference between the drug testing programs of parochial schools and public schools, according to the statement by Harry Connick?
2. What percentage of students tested positive in the first year of the drug testing program at De La Salle High School, according to the statement by Yvonne Gelpi? What percentage of students tested positive in the third year?
3. How soon after the drug testing program began at De La Salle High School was Aaron Middleberg able to notice the reduction in peer pressure to take drugs?

*J*ohn L. Mica, chairman, Subcommittee on Criminal Justice, Drug Policy, and Human Resources. Today's hearing is being conducted at the request of Mr. Vitter, and the order of business today will be, I will start with an opening statement. . . .

This being an investigations and oversight subcommittee of Congress, for the benefit of the witnesses testifying today, all of the witnesses will be sworn. I will do that in just a minute. . . .

Today, we are focusing on the special challenges and threats facing New Orleans. Drugs pose a threat to our schools, to our law enforcement officials, and also to your health system. Since, again, New Orleans is so strategically located between the southwest border and the eastern seaboard, your community faces a great risk that drug trafficking organizations will operate here to move drugs coming in from Mexico and South America, the Caribbean and to and from other parts of the United States. . . .

I am going to first recognize the district attorney of New Orleans, State of Louisiana, Mr. Harry Connick, for his statement. Good morning. . . .

Statement of District Attorney Harry Connick

Mr. Connick. Good morning. I must begin by thanking you, Congressman Mica, for authorizing and chairing the subcommittee hearing, and Congressman David Vitter for requesting it and making it happen. Thanks are also due to our Congressman William Jefferson and our Senator Mary Landrieu for their interest and support of our high school drug testing efforts. . . .

The majority of tax dollars being spent to combat illegal drugs are spent trying to reduce the supply side of drug trade. However, there will always be a supply if there is a need. Only relatively recently has serious thought been given to the critical need for testing, treatment and counseling, the best way to reduce drug demand. Fortunately, increased attention is being given to programs that deal with drug users coming into the criminal justice system. Diversion programs and drug courts are beginning to show signs of success. But these efforts are directed to persons who are already a part of the criminal justice system.

The question we should now seriously address is, how do we keep people, especially teenagers out of the system? We have learned that there is one method that stands out as the most effective prevention method today, and that is drug testing. In the New Orleans area, we are now using the most effective demand-reduction tool, I believe, that this country has ever known, and that is the testing of a limited number of our high school students in this area. We have learned, through concrete, tangible experience that drug testing is working. In New Orleans alone, there are currently [2009] three parochial high schools successfully testing all of their students, three more parochial high schools in St. Tammany Parish are doing the same, and three additional parochial high schools in Jefferson Parish will begin testing this fall.

These schools utilize drug testing by use of hair analysis, which we have found to be the most effective testing method. Other schools, both public and private, want to implement drug testing programs, but cannot do so because of an absence of funds. Public schools in New Orleans will begin testing the 3-percent of all students engaging in athletic and other extra-curricular activities this fall. Probably the most significant and dramatic event taking place in New Orleans is the planned drug testing of public school students at Frederick A.

In schools that conduct random drug tests, almost all tested athletes, and more than half tested students who participate in nonathletic extracurricular activities. Just 28.4 percent tested the entire student body.

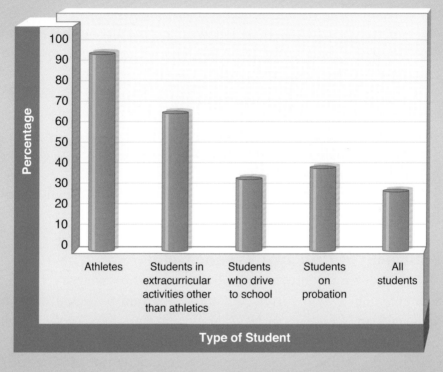

Taken from: Chris Ringwalt, et al. "Random Drug Testing in US Public School Districts," *American Journal of Public Health*, vol. 98, no. 5, May 2008, p. 827.

Douglass High School. Douglass is the first and only public school to adopt such a unique drug testing program, employing both the 3-percent rule and the voluntary testing of students. Mr. Vincent Nzinga is the principal at that school. The Douglass program will begin this fall, and will run for a 2-year period.

There are many benefits to drug testing high school students, who incidentally probably will have to be tested anyway after they leave school. First, testing identifies those students using drugs, and is the predicate for early intervention in the form of non-punitive counseling and treatment. It also deters the use of drugs, especially among those students who are beginning to consider experimenting with drugs, and it is a fact that most students refuse to use drugs when they know they are going to be tested. Also students who remain drug-free until their 18th year will probably not use drugs thereafter, and it is certainly less expensive to drug test and treat a person before arrest than after.

Parents are overwhelmingly in support of having their children tested. We know drug testing reduces demand, and when you reduce the demand, supply reduction must follow. There is a dire need to expand these successful drug-testing programs, and we are looking to you to lead the way in funding these projects.

We thank you for visiting us and urge you to help us in Louisiana to create a model high school drug testing reduction program for the country. Thank you.

Mr. Mica. Thank you. And we will withhold questions until we have heard from all of the witnesses.

The next witness is the president and principal of the high school here, Yvonne Gelpi. You are recognized. . . .

Statement of Principal Yvonne Gelpi

Ms. Gelpi. Good morning, Chairman Mica; welcome back, Congressman David Vitter. We are very proud of David, he was valedictorian of his class of 1979, graduated from De La Salle [High School, New Orleans, LA], and distinguished guests.

What if I told you I had a way to reduce detentions for fighting by 85 percent, and detentions for disruptive behavior by 65 percent in your schools? What if I told you you could completely turn around the culture of your schools, reducing stealing and cheating, so that students could focus on getting their educations? If I told you it would cost about $50 a student to accomplish this, would you object? Would any parent object to this additional cost?

De La Salle has found a way to accomplish this, and it happens when a school does mandatory drug testing of students, faculty and staff. We are not talking theory here, we are not talking possibilities, we are speaking about hard data, gathered from over 2,500 drug tests over a 3-year period. We did reduce detentions. We did change the culture of our school. But better than that, we gave our students a chance to say no to peer pressure and to avoid experimentation with drugs at a young age.

In the Youth Risk Behavior Survey by the Louisiana Office of Addictive Disorders, conducted prior to our implementation of mandatory drug testing, we found that 10 percent of our students reported trying marijuana and 10 percent trying cocaine before the age of 13. Frightening. Thirty percent indicated they had been offered, sold or given illegal drugs on our campus.

The purpose of our drug testing program is not intended to be punitive. It is intended to stop an undesirable behavior that is interfering with learning. We warned our students 90 days before the tests began that, if they were experimenting with drugs, they should cease immediately. We wanted to throw out the drugs, not the kids.

On the handout on page 2, are some statistics about our program over a 3-year period. Year one, we had 3.4 percent test positive. Year two, positives were down to 2.1. And year three, the latest results, which are not even printed in the booklet yet, the number is fewer than 1 percent. That is 6 students out of 850; 5 of them seniors and 1 junior; 5 boys and 1 girl. The results speak for themselves. Mandatory drug testing works. . . .

Mr. Mica. Thank you for your testimony. And we will hear now from Aaron Middleberg. He is a former student of De La Salle High School. You are recognized, sir.

Statement of Former Student Aaron Middleberg

Mr. Middleberg. Good morning, Chairman Mica, Congressman Vitter, and guests. My name is Aaron Middleberg, and I am a graduate of De La Salle's class of 1999.

I came to De La Salle in 1995 as a freshman. Two years into my high school career, De La Salle introduced the drug testing policies.

The witnesses giving their statements in this viewpoint suggest that it is not just athletes or those who participate in extracurricular activities who should be tested for drugs, but rather every student in the school.

All students were informed that in 90 days, the entire student body would receive a drug test. This came as a bit of a surprise to several students and parents, but the administration knew the challenges the students faced, and the fact that drugs were readily available in the New Orleans area. And this would be a way to make sure that each student was taking full advantage of the right to learn in a safe and drug-free environment.

The administration moved through with their plan and drug tested the entire student body. Barely 2 months after the drug testing began, I was called down to Ms. Gelpi's office. I thought to myself, what have I possibly done now? I knew I had parked in the teachers' lot, as well as probably was tardy, and I just might have cut in the lunch line. But I was wrong. It was not for those reasons. She wanted my opinion on the drug testing. My answer to her was, I think it has been wonderful. The people that would hang around outside of school when the dismissal bell would ring were gone, and the No. 1 thing that made a difference was, every single student in

De La Salle had a reason to say no. Every De La Salle student had a reason to say no.

One might ask, is it worth the money to drug test everyone, or should we just drug test the kids we suspect? Test every single person, including the staff, and you will have a school that is almost drug-free, and one less peer pressure on a student—one less peer pressure.

It worked for me, so let us make it work for everyone. It is not a punishment, it is a privilege to know someone cares that much about you.

Thank you. . . .

> ## EVALUATING THE AUTHOR'S ARGUMENTS:
>
> Compare the arguments presented by the witnesses in this viewpoint, who support drug testing every student, with those of the author of the following viewpoint, Jennifer Kern, who argues that no student should be tested for drugs. With which viewpoint do you agree more? Explain your answer using evidence from each viewpoint.

No Student Should Be Drug Tested

Jennifer Kern

"Student drug testing programs are invasive, unproven, expensive and, perhaps most important, potentially counter-productive."

In the following viewpoint Jennifer Kern argues that athletes are not the only students who should not be subject to random drug testing—*no* student should be drug tested, in her opinion. Kern cites data that show little difference in drug use between students who go to schools that test for drugs and those who do not. She warns that random drug testing programs not only fail to keep students off drugs and alienate them from drug-preventative extracurricular activities, but they also may encourage students to try drugs that do not show up on drug tests, or to abuse alcohol. Kern concludes that drug education and counseling programs are a better answer to the problem of student drug use than random student drug testing programs.

Kern is a research associate at the Drug Policy Alliance and coauthor of the 2006 report "Making Sense of Student Drug Testing: Why Educators Are Saying No," published by the American Civil Liberties Union and the Drug Policy Alliance.

1. What did researchers from Oregon Health and Science University find about random drug and alcohol testing programs, according to Kern?
2. With what does the author say a school district in Ohio replaced its drug testing program?
3. What, in Kern's opinion, is counterproductive about banning students who test positive for drug use from after-school activities?

T he White House Office of National Drug Control Policy descends upon Washington state Thursday and Friday to host two summits designed to entice local educators to start drug testing students—randomly and without cause.

Random drug testing in schools, made a priority by the Bush administration, may not fly in this state, as the Washington Supreme Court is considering a challenge to the policy under the higher privacy protections of the state constitution. However, objections go beyond constitutional concerns. Student drug testing programs are invasive, unproven, expensive and, perhaps most important, potentially counterproductive.

Drug testing is invasive and the collection of a specimen can be especially alienating to adolescents. Schools must ask students to disclose private medical information regarding their prescription medications to try to control for false positives, raising additional anxieties—among students and faculty—about the potential for breaches in confidentiality and false accusations.

Random student drug testing programs are unproven. The American Academy of Pediatrics' policy statement says, "There is little evidence of the effectiveness of school-based drug testing in the scientific literature." In fact, the only national, peer-reviewed study conducted on the topic compared 94,000 students in almost 900 U.S. schools with and without a drug testing program, and found virtually no difference in illegal drug use. Last November, researchers from Oregon Health and Science University published research findings from randomized experimental trials that found random drug and alcohol testing did not reliably reduce past-month drug and alcohol use among student athletes.

For its high price tag, testing is inefficient in detecting drug problems. Though it may provide a false sense of security among school officials and parents, testing detects only a tiny fraction of users and misses too many who might be in real trouble. The Dublin School District in Ohio abandoned its $35,000 drug-testing program and instead hired two full-time substance abuse counselors.

Finally, and perhaps most troubling, there is evidence that random drug testing programs are counterproductive. The researchers from OHSU found attitudinal changes among students in schools with drug testing programs that indicate new risk factors for future substance use. Student athletes in schools with drug testing reported less positive attitudes toward school, less faith in the benefits of drug testing and less belief that testing was a reason not to use drugs, among other indicators. Those findings support objections that suspicionless testing can erode relationships of trust between students and adults at school, damaging an essential component of a safe and rewarding learning environment.

There are numerous other potential unintended consequences of random student drug testing programs. Testing erects counterproductive barriers to participation in extracurricular activities—the very activities that provide structure and supervision during the peak hours of adolescent drug use from 3–6 p.m. Testing may also trigger oppositional behavior, such as trying to "beat" the test. The American Academy of Pediatrics warns that mandatory testing may inadvertently encour-

> **FAST FACT**
>
> According to the American Civil Liberties Union, readily available, commonly used, and legal substances—such as over-the-counter cold medications and foods containing poppy seeds—can cause students to falsely test positive for illegal drugs such as amphetamines, LSD, and opiates.

"Board of Education v. Earls," cartoon by Stu's Views. Reprinted with permission of Stu's Views. © Stu Rees. www.stus.com.

age more students to abuse alcohol—not included in many standard testing panels—or may motivate some drug-involved adolescents to switch to harder drugs that leave the system more quickly.

We would better serve young people by facing the reality that there is no quick fix for the complex issues surrounding substance abuse. Random drug testing, such as the "Just Say No" approach, oversimplifies the complexities of life teenagers face these days.

Instead of investing in surveillance, we should spend our time and resources educating students through comprehensive, interactive and honest drug education with identification of, and assistance for, students whose lives are disrupted by substance use.

EVALUATING THE AUTHOR'S ARGUMENTS:

To make her argument Jennifer Kern warns that drug testing programs may actually encourage students to try drugs that are not detectable by tests. Think about drug use and drug testing (if applicable) at your school. In your opinion, does your school have a drug problem? Are students tested for drugs? If so, do you think the testing program encourages or prevents drug use? If students are not tested at your school, do you think a testing program would help or hurt students? Use examples to back up your ideas.

Chapter 3

How Does Drug Testing Affect the School Community?

A laboratory technician inserts a tube containing a urine specimen into a mixing device to ensure an even and complete mix prior to a steroid test.

Drug Testing Discourages Student Participation in School Activities

Allie Brody

> *"Students shouldn't be forced to choose between their principles and their favorite school club."*

In the following viewpoint Allie Brody argues against mandatory student drug testing because it discourages students from participating in extracurricular activities. Brody explains that she was very active in her high school's extracurricular program— she was part of the school newspaper and the French Honor Society and cofounded the school's first philosophy club, among other activities. But then her school made a rule that any student who participates in extracurricular activities must submit to a drug test. Brody thought the drug tests were humiliating, an invasion of privacy, and a potential threat to students. So she refused to be tested, only to be informed that she could not participate in extra-curricular activities unless she did so. In

Brody's opinion, this is counterproductive—students interested in participating in clubs, athletics, and other activities should not have to submit to a drug test in order to so. She warns that fewer students will participate in extracurricular activities to avoid being drug tested, and she concludes that lower participation is bad for students and the school. Brody is cofounder of the group Students Morally Against Random Testing (SMART).

AS YOU READ, CONSIDER THE FOLLOWING QUESTIONS:
1. What is an "extracurricular exile," according to the author?
2. What is the American Academy of Pediatrics' position on student drug testing, according to Brody?
3. What activities did the student opposition group cofounded by Brody conduct while her school considered adopting a random student drug testing policy?

The piece of advice I heard most often before entering, and during, high school came in two words: "get involved." Extracurricular activities, I was told, give students a chance to better the school, meet new people and make the most of their four years. I took the advice to heart and got involved in numerous ways: I've written for my school newspaper, helped out with the production of musicals and even traveled abroad through a school club. I was later inducted into the French Honor Society and the National Honor Society. Last year [in 2008], I even co-founded the school's first philosophy club.

An "Extracurricular Exile"

But this year I am barred from participating in any of it. The irony is that my school has made me ineligible for any extracurricular activity for what they believe is my own self-interest. What did I do to deserve this punishment? I acted on my principles and stood up for fairness, privacy and dignity for me and my fellow students. My school's reaction to me taking a moral position was to make me an "extracurricular exile."

You see, over the summer my high school passed a mandatory random student drug-testing policy. The [George W.] Bush administration

Students who do not participate in drug testing may be banned from a school's extracurricular activities, such as the school band.

had been pushing this policy to schools across the country. It forces students who participate in extracurricular activities to submit to humiliating drug tests—randomly and without cause. Instead of improving the drug education and counseling capacity in our schools, the former administration chose scare tactics and unproven zero-tolerance methods. Hopefully the [Barack] Obama administration, which has already shown its support for evidence-based practices on a number of issues, will rethink support of random student drug testing, so other students don't have to go through what I did.

Taking Action Against a Bad Policy

It should be common sense that scaring students won't help them any to make smarter decisions. The American Academy of Pediatrics

[AAP] provides all the evidence one needs. In a policy statement, the AAP cautions that student drug testing is unsupported by scientific research and carries inherent dangers. Drug-testing programs break down trust between students and administrators. They also carry the inherent danger of motivating some students to switch to drugs that will leave the system quickly, like alcohol, or drugs that will not show up in the tests, such as inhalants and herbal concoctions.

Last year, when I found out my school board was considering a random student drug-testing policy, I immediately began organizing a student opposition group. We worked to get the community involved: Students joined with parents and teachers, donning "Drug Testing Fails Our Youth" T-shirts as we filed into the school board meetings.

We even brought a toxicologist to speak with the board about the unreliable nature of the drug-testing technology, the problem of non-professionals interpreting the test results, privacy and legal-liability issues and the general lack of research supporting student drug testing. To us it seemed the school's arguments in favor of testing were based more on emotional rhetoric than data. But, in the end, emotion carried the day, and random student drug testing went forward.

Forcing Students to Choose

My parents and I understand that my school is trying to help students stay safe. But we also believe this policy is the wrong approach. Perhaps worst of all, the policy overrules the judgment of my parents, who do not want to submit their child to this invasive program. I feel it is my civic duty to hold on tight to the freedom that defines

"It's for passing my drug test," cartoon by McCoy, Glenn and Gary. www.CartoonStock.com. Copyright © McCoy, Glenn and Gary. Reproduction rights obtainable from www.CartoonStock.com.

our great country. In fulfilling this duty, I am giving up my extracurricular activities in order to maintain my principles. I hope under the new administration we can stop the spread of these programs and redirect our scarce education dollars toward counseling and honest drug education and prevention.

Other students shouldn't be forced to choose between their principles and their favorite school club.

Drug Testing Does Not Discourage Student Participation in School Activities

C.E. Edwards

"[Drug testing] programs contribute to a nurturing environment that allows students to flourish and to participate in the educational process."

In the following viewpoint C.E. Edwards argues that drug testing programs do not discourage students from participating in extracurricular activities. Edwards examines data from the New Jersey Department of Education that compared attendance rates, suspension rates, expulsion rates, drop-out rates, graduation rates, test score performances, and other measures of student involvement in those schools with drug testing programs and those without them. She reports that schools with drug testing programs enjoy higher attendance, higher graduation rates, and higher test scores. Schools without testing programs, however, have higher suspension, drop-out, and expulsion rates. The author concludes that mandatory student drug testing does not discourage students from participating in school activities—if anything, she says, students in drug testing schools thrive and participate more than students at schools without such programs.

Edwards is a member of the Student Drug Testing Coalition, a project of the Drug-Free Projects Coalition, Inc., which provides school districts with information that helps them implement student drug testing programs.

AS YOU READ, CONSIDER THE FOLLOWING QUESTIONS:
1. What does Edwards say attendance rates are in schools with and without drug testing programs?
2. How do graduation rates compare in New Jersey schools with drug testing programs and in those without, according to the author?
3. How many students does Edwards say were expelled from schools with drug testing programs versus from schools without such programs?

M aking the decision to add a student random drug-testing program (RSDT) to existing prevention programs should be based upon factual and accurate information, while also benefitting from the experience of more than 16 percent of U.S. secondary school districts that have implemented student drug testing programs. Factual information on student drug-testing programs is widely available, yet districts and parents considering such programs continue to be subjected to a litany of claims that RSDT programs negatively impact student morale and behaviors without any supporting evidence. When closely examined, these claims are found to be conjecture or worse, opinion offered as fact and unsubstantiated by data.

Criticisms of Drug Testing Programs Are Unsupported

In a review of data from the New Jersey Department of Education and individual school districts with similar demographics for the 2006–2007 school year, conducted by [New Jersey high school principal] Christina Steffner, it was found that when comparing schools with RSDT programs to schools without programs, claims of negative impacts were unsupported. At least three additional studies have also found no evidence that RSDT programs negatively impact students.

Many school districts across the U.S. have access to state report-card data similar to what is available in New Jersey. Such data can be compiled and analyzed to determine if student morale and behaviors have been negatively impacted in those districts with RSDT programs while considering the following list of frequently-cited and unsubstantiated claims of negative impacts.

Those opposing RSDT programs conjecture that such programs will:

- Decrease levels of participation in extra-curricular and after-school activities
- Create distrust between students and teachers
- Create distrust between students and administrators
- Create distrust between students and parents
- Create a school atmosphere of resentment, suspicion and alienation
- Increase truancy rates
- Cause drug-use diversion to less-detectable drugs
- Breach student confidentiality if prescribed medications used
- Invade student privacy rights
- Provide a false sense of a drug-free environment
- Allow for identification of drug use without providing for a remedy
- Use school resources that should be used for education

Are these opinions supported by fact? A review of school data in New Jersey clearly demonstrates such claims of negative impacts are unsupported. In reality, the data review provides evidence to the contrary, supporting clear evidence of a positive impact at those schools with RSDT programs. . . .

Testing Schools Stay Connected to Students

The overall findings in New Jersey demonstrated that daily attendance rates at schools with RSDT programs (94.8%) were higher than at non-RSDT schools (89.8%). Graduation rates were also higher at schools with RSDT (96%) than for students enrolled at non-testing schools (95.4%). Students subject to RSDT scored higher, on average, on the High School Proficiency Assessment (HSPA) and the

SAT. The data also demonstrates that more students from RSDT districts go on to higher education (90.9%) as compared to their counterparts in non-testing districts (89.3%). Suspension and drop-out rates were lower at schools with RSDT programs. While there was only one expulsion at a RSDT school, non-testing schools had 14 expulsions. This data clearly refutes assertions that students attending schools with RSDT programs experience a loss of connectedness with their schools as measured by indicators such as student performance on standardized tests, daily attendance, graduation, suspension, expulsion and dropout rates.

Hunterdon Central Regional High School, randomly drug testing students since 1996, has an enrollment of just under 3200 students in grades 9–12. The statistical data from Hunterdon Central Regional High School, as well as that for the other 25 RSDT New Jersey high schools, clearly demonstrates that student participation in athletics or extra-curricular activities did not decrease. This data also serves to refute the related conjecture that risky behaviors, resulting from decreased participation, will increase.

No Increase in Truancy or Decrease in Participation

Student participation in activities was consistent among schools of similar demographics and locales with non-RSDT schools reporting similar levels of participation. . . .

As to creating an environment of resentment, distrust and suspicion between parent-child and/or school-child relationships leading to a loss of school connectedness and runaway behavior, the schools with RSDT programs showed no increase in runaway or truancy behaviors when compared to schools without programs.

New Jersey school districts, through the use of research based studies such as the Rocky Mountain Behavioral Science Institute American Drug and Alcohol Survey, did not experience drug-use diversion to less detectable or non-tested drugs. Most districts construct RSDT policies that permit testing for a variety of substances and modification of the drug-test panels. Many districts also allow for a variety of specimens that may be collected and tested, randomly selecting specimen type when the student reports for testing. Students, therefore, cannot be certain what drugs will be included in the test, nor do they have the opportunity to substitute specimens.

Student Privacy Is Always Protected

Using proven and generally-accepted procedures and practices for any drug-testing program prevents breaching student confidentiality and privacy. Standard procedures include un-observed collections when the specimen is urine. Many districts contract for specimen collection with a third party. A necessary part of any correctly-structured RSDT program is the use of a Medical Review Officer (MRO). A licensed physician, the MRO is specifically trained to interpret drug-test results and reviews all positive test results. Where there is a question of legitimate use of a prescription drug, the MRO makes direct contact with a parent and obtains prescription medication information. The MRO verifies legitimate use of the substance and reports the drug-test result as 'negative' to the school representative.

U.S. public school districts with RSDT programs must adhere to specific requirements of student confidentiality as dictated by The Federal Privacy Act, The Federal Alcohol and Drug Abuse Act and Federal Regulation. Students are not identified by name, social security number, or student identification number for drug-test purposes. All drug-testing records are maintained separate from permanent records and must be destroyed upon graduation. School district officials may not share information of a positive screen with local law enforcement agencies. Information on drug-test results may only be given to the student and the parent. Only individuals authorized to administer the program are permitted access to drug-test results.

All schools included in this review, as well as most others in the U.S., recognize that RSDT is only one part of a comprehensive prevention strategy that should also include drug and alcohol education programs. New Jersey public schools with RSDT programs continue to utilize multi-faceted prevention strategies to meet the annual state-mandated 10 hours of drug and alcohol education for grades K–12. Campuses are not promoted as drug-free environments—but those with RSDT programs are certainly shown to be environments that maintain a clear and strong message that drug use by students is unacceptable.

Drug-Tested Students Flourish and Participate

New Jersey schools offer Student Assistance Programs and Student Assistance Counselors on staff as a remedy and support when there is student drug use. These professionals provide education and counseling for students who test positive. While most students do not require treatment, district policies require students who have a positive-test result to be evaluated by a licensed drug addictions counselor and to follow any recommendations made by the counselor.

Testing Programs Encourage Student Participation

A 2008 study compared attendance rates, suspension rates, graduation rates, and other factors among New Jersey high schools with random drug testing programs and those without. It found that schools with drug testing programs enjoyed higher attendance rates, graduation rates, and higher test scores. Schools without drug testing programs had higher suspension, drop-out, and expulsion rates.

	= Higher Value	Non-testing Schools	Schools with Drug Testing Programs
Total number of schools		26	26
Total enrollment		39,184	37,923
Daily attendance rate		89.8%	94.8%
Graduation rate		95.4%	96%
Suspension rate		15.9%	11%
Dropout rate		1.1%	0.9%
Number of Expulsions		14	1
Students passing state standardized tests		91.6%	95.2%
Average math, language arts, SATs		505/489	511/496
Students going on to higher education		89.3%	90.9%

Taken from: C.E. Edwards, "Student Drug-Testing Programs: Do These Programs Negatively Impact Students?," Drug-Free Projects Coalition, Inc., July 2008.

Those schools not using a third-party collector, train school nurses or designated staff to administer the RSDT program. Teachers continue their work as educators and are not generally involved in RSDT programs. The cost of a RSDT program can be budgeted to meet the needs of the school district without taking time or funds from the primary role of education. School districts in New Jersey and across the U.S. have found ways to raise or re-allocate funds, obtain grant funding or other means of supporting RSDT programs. School time and resources are not diverted from the primary mission of education to administer a RSDT program.

The use of research-based and local Organizational Health Inventories (OHI) satisfaction tools, review and analysis of state report-card data used to measure performance indicators of schools and discussion with school officials in New Jersey provide clear evidence that refutes the claims of negative effects of RSDT on students and school culture. Schools with RSDT programs send a clear message about drug and alcohol use, provide students with opportunities to avoid drug and alcohol use, provide a means for identification and early intervention in student drug and alcohol use. These programs contribute to a nurturing environment that allows students to flourish and to participate in the educational process.

EVALUATING THE AUTHOR'S ARGUMENTS:

To make her argument that student drug testing programs do not discourage participation, C.E. Edwards reports on data collected from fifty-two New Jersey high schools that reflected the behaviors of 77,107 students. Do you think this is a large enough sample to make definitive statements about the effect of drug testing programs on student participation? If yes, why? If no, why not, and what kind of sample would you prefer to see?

Mandatory Student Drug Testing Reduces Drug Use

"Illegal use of drugs among our high school students is being reduced—a positive step no matter how small a decline."

James T. Jeffers

In the following viewpoint James T. Jeffers argues that drug testing programs are effective at reducing drug use among student populations. He uses his own school system as an example of a successful drug testing program. Since the schools in his county began testing students for drugs, they have seen drug use decline among high school students. Middle school students have tested clean for drugs. In addition, Jeffers has not seen evidence that participation in athletics or other extracurricular activities has declined as a result of the testing program. He concludes that mandatory student drug testing programs successfully reduce drug use without harming students or schools.

Jeffers is superintendent of the Tallassee City Schools in Tallassee, Alabama.

AS YOU READ, CONSIDER THE FOLLOWING QUESTIONS:
1. What does Jeffers say is the number one problem facing students in Tallassee, Alabama?
2. By what percentage did drug use go down among ninth to twelfth graders who participated in a drug testing program, according to the author?
3. How many seventh and eighth graders does Jeffers say have tested positive for drugs in the two years since Tallassee began its drug testing program?

Rather than being radical and polarizing, random student drug testing has been embraced by students, parents, teachers and others in our community of Tallassee, Ala., as an effective supplement to what we teach in the classroom.

Random student drug testing reinforces every other prevention program in our school by supporting the no-use standard with testing that is linked to nonpunitive consequences. Our experience shows that student drug testing does not put kids out of school or out of athletics and other extracurricular activities. It is the use of drugs and alcohol that does that.

Drug Testing Addresses a Serious Problem

Rather than invading students' privacy and driving a wedge between students and adults, the drug testing has actually built trust based on verified test results. At our 612-student high school, the No. 1 issue facing today's teens is substance abuse, including recreational drugs, marijuana, methamphetamine, steroids, over-the-counter medication, prescription drugs and, of course, tobacco and alcohol.

Tallassee City Schools began its random student drug testing program in 2002. At the time, we encountered a widely held perception among the stakeholders that a huge problem with drug use existed at our middle school and high school. To address the reality, I formed a committee to study the issue of student drug use in our school district and to develop an action plan to reduce the problem.

The committee consisted of school administrators, parents, athletic coaches, cheerleader sponsors, teachers, board of education members, city leaders, club sponsors, band personnel, a doctor, nurses, police and others. The 35 invited members began by looking at nationwide data regarding random student drug testing and the legal aspects of drug tests. The committee met once a month for the first four months of the year.

A Legal and Well-Designed Program

After examining the facts, the committee was convinced the Tallassee City Schools should implement random drug testing of our students to demonstrate to the public the seriousness of our actions. The next question was what should be in the policy. The committee turned to other schools in Alabama that already were randomly testing. We borrowed written policies from the Hoover, Ala., schools and the Hartselle, Ala., schools, two school systems that had won court approval in our state.

The committee adopted what we considered the best practices of the two policies and developed our own policy for Tallassee. The board of education passed it unanimously. When the proposed policy was introduced at two consecutive school board meetings, no one in the audience presented negative reactions either in written or oral form.

> **FAST FACT**
>
> According to the Office of National Drug Control Policy, a case study in Alabama's Autauga County School System showed that student drug testing accounted for a reduction in marijuana use from 18.5 percent to 11.8 percent.

The new drug prevention policy was implemented in fall 2002 and was included in the Student Code of Conduct and Information Handbook, which is available to all stakeholders through the district's website.

The student drug testing program has been well received and universally supported in the community. The policy has not been challenged to date and no legal action has been threatened.

Successful Results

Several measures have demonstrated the positive effects of the random student drug testing in our schools. The first and most important statistic is that since the first two years of drug testing, 7th and 8th graders have been testing clean. That alone has demonstrated the impact of the prevention program. Other collected data show a reduction in drug use of more than 30 percent during the past three years among students in grades 9–12. We have participated with the Institute of Behavior and Health, a federal contractor in Rockville, Md. and other school systems to gather long-term data on drug testing of students.

The most impressive measure of success is the perception that Tallassee City Schools is doing something effective to help students who test positive for drugs. The most significant benefit is the new perception that illegal use of drugs among our high school students is being reduced—a positive step no matter how small a decline and worth the cost of drug testing.

During the past two years, we've had no positive test results among our 7th and 8th graders and a general decline in usage among high school students.

Dr. Linn Goldberg, cofounder of the Atlas and Athena Drug Prevention Programs, meets with National Football League players from the Washington Redskins. Players are participating in the program, which also includes participation by Tallassee, Alabama, schools.

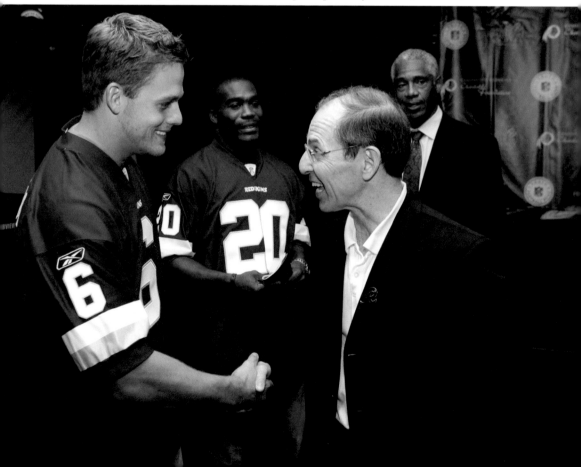

Good for Students, Good for Communities

In addition to the drug testing, the Tallassee City Schools also has participated in the national prevention education programs—Atlas for boys and Athena for girls who are involved in interscholastic athletics. These programs were implemented with a grant from the Institute of Behavior and Health in cooperation with the Oregon Health [and Science] University.

These programs prepare peer teachers (usually sports coaches or club sponsors) to discuss all aspects of student health, including use of drugs and steroids and healthy eating. Students spend time in groups discussing the pressures they face each day and how to make healthy choices.

When the school district last winter had vacancies for athletic director and head football coach, the school board unanimously supported a search for an individual who would fully embrace random student drug testing in Tallassee.

For those of us in leadership, the random student drug testing is an expression of our concern for our students and our commitment to helping them grow up as drug-free, healthy and productive adults. The experience in Tallassee has been positive for our students, their families, our school and our community.

> **EVALUATING THE AUTHOR'S ARGUMENTS:**
>
> James T. Jeffers, the author of this viewpoint, is a school superintendent. Does the fact that he has personal experience with schools, students, and drug testing programs make you more likely to agree with his position that testing programs reduce drug use among students? If so, why? If not, why not?

Mandatory Student Drug Testing Does Not Significantly Reduce Drug Use

"If all that testing accomplishes is that 6 percent of football players or glee club members start smoking pot less often, the payoff hardly seems worth the cost."

Jacob Sullum

In the following viewpoint Jacob Sullum argues that mandatory student drug testing does not significantly reduce drug use. He discusses a 2010 study by the US Department of Education that found that student drug testing programs are only slightly effective. Although such programs were found to reduce student drug use, they did not do so by much. Sullum reports that the difference in drug use at schools with testing programs and those without came down to a few percentage points. Furthermore, tested students said that they were more likely to use drugs in the future than students at schools without testing programs, indicating that their general view on drugs was not affected by the presence of testing. Finally, students who were tested regarded the consequences of drug use similarly to their nontested counterparts. Sullum concludes that drug testing programs have an insignificant impact on student drug use and are not worth the money, the effort, and the violation of students' privacy.

Sullum is a nationally syndicated columnist and a senior editor at *Reason* magazine, the flagship publication of the Reason Foundation, a libertarian think tank based in Los Angeles.

AS YOU READ, CONSIDER THE FOLLOWING QUESTIONS:
1. What, in the author's opinion, is the difference between saying "six percentage points" and "a 27 percent decline"?
2. What percentage of tested students said they "definitely will" or "probably will" use substances in the next twelve months, according to Sullum?
3. What impact does Sullum say drug testing programs have on school disciplinary incidents?

During the last decade, with encouragement (and financial assistance) from the federal government, the share of school districts that randomly test students for drugs has nearly tripled, from about 5 percent to 14 percent. According to the Supreme Court, such testing is constitutional as a condition for participating in sports and other extracurricular activities, and the logic of these rulings suggests it would also be constitutional if imposed on the entire student body. But is it effective? A new Education Department report supplies an answer: not very.

That conclusion is based on a study in which 36 high schools were randomly assigned to a "treatment" group, which meant they began testing students during the 2007–08 school year, or to a "control" group, which meant they delayed drug testing until after the study was completed in the spring of 2008. For advocates of testing, the most impressive finding is that 16 percent of students subject to spot urine checks, when surveyed in 2008, reported using drugs in the previous month, compared to 22 percent of students participating in the same

A 2010 study by the US Department of Education found that student drug testing programs are only slightly effective in reducing drug use.

activities at schools that did not have drug testing. Some of this difference may be due to a reduced willingness of students whose urine is under surveillance to be candid about their drug use. In any case, the difference is only six percentage points, although it sounds more impressive if you call it, as supporters of testing surely will, a 27 percent decline in drug use. They also can cite this study as evidence that drug testing does not discourage participation in extracurricular activities.

But here are some other things this study did not find:

Are students who are subject to MRSDT [mandatory random student drug testing] less likely to report that they will use illicit substances in the future than comparable students in high schools without MRSDT?

No, 34 percent of students subject to MRSDT reported that they "definitely will" or "probably will" use substances in the next 12 months, compared with 33 percent of comparable students in schools without MRSDT.

Do students who are subject to MRSDT report different perceptions of the consequences of substance use than comparable students in high schools without MRSDT?

No, on two measures of students' perceptions of the positive and negative consequences of using substances, students subject to MRSDT did not report having different perceptions of the consequences of substance use relative to comparable students in high schools without MRSDT. . . .

Does the MRSDT program have spillover effects on the substance use or other outcomes of students who are not covered by the MRSDT policies?

No, the MRSDT program had no spillover effects. For example, 36 percent of students not covered by the MRSDT policy in treatment schools and 36 percent of comparable students in control schools reported using a substance in the past 30 days.

> # FAST FACT
>
> A 2003 study by researchers at the University of Michigan titled "Drug Testing in Schools" showed that the prevalence of marijuana use by students subject to random drug testing was approximately 94.7 percent; the prevalence of marijuana use by students not subject to random drug testing was approximately 95 percent.

Does the MRSDT program affect the number of disciplinary incidents reported by schools?

No, the MRSDT program had no impact on school-reported disciplinary incidents. For example, treatment schools reported an average of five instances per 1,000 students of distribution, possession, or use of illegal drugs compared with four such instances in control schools.

Here are the conclusions I draw from this evidence:

1. Teenagers, like adults, are willing to trade their urine for things they value.
2. The threat of losing that benefit deters them, to some extent, from using drugs.

Drug Testing Has No Long-Term Benefits

A 2010 study by the US Department of Education found that drug testing students did not make them less likely to use drugs in the future.

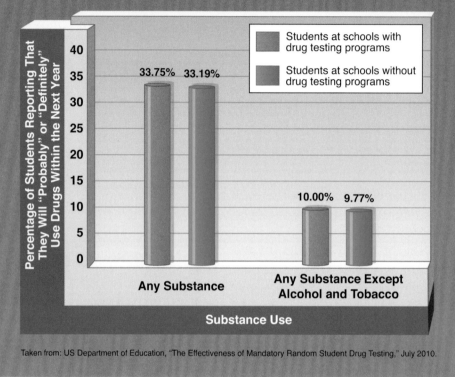

Taken from: US Department of Education, "The Effectiveness of Mandatory Random Student Drug Testing," July 2010.

3. That does not mean they have suddenly seen the light about the virtues of a drug-free life, as shown by the fact that they are no more likely to take a negative view of drugs and no less likely to plan on using drugs in the future.

4. Not surprisingly, the plainly goal-oriented abstinence of students participating in extracurricular activities has no modeling effect on other students, who don't see anything to gain from keeping drug metabolites out of their urine.

Most important, there is no evidence that the measured reduction in drug use among students subject to testing has prevented any real-world problems (such as "disciplinary incidents"). If all that testing accomplishes is that 6 percent of football players or glee club members start smoking pot less often, the payoff hardly seems worth the cost in terms of money, effort, and indignity. Worse, these programs train students to go along with the government's arbitrary requirements, sacrifice their privacy on the slightest pretext, and keep their reservations to themselves while secretly maintaining politically incorrect attitudes. These are not the habits of a free society.

EVALUATING THE AUTHORS' ARGUMENTS:

Jacob Sullum cites data that show drug tested students were no more likely to avoid drugs in the future, no more likely to inspire their peers to be drug free, and no less likely to have drug-related disciplinary incidents. Yet he admits that, overall, the data show that students at schools with drug testing programs use drugs at a lower rate than students at schools without drug testing programs. In light of these mixed results, are you more likely to conclude that drug testing programs reduce or have no significant effect on student drug use? Explain your reasoning and quote from the texts you have read in this book to support your conclusions.

Drug Testing Encourages the Use of Other Drugs

Tom Angell

"There is evidence suggesting drug testing actually exacerbates the problem of teen drug abuse."

In the following viewpoint Tom Angell argues that student drug testing programs worsen the problem of teen drug abuse. He explains that testing programs encourage students to experiment with drugs that are not detected by drug tests. Oftentimes, says Angell, these drugs are harder, or more dangerous, than the drugs they would otherwise have used. He says it is counterproductive to ban students who test positive, or to ban students who refuse to be tested, from afterschool activities. He reports that research shows that teen drug use is highest in the after-school hours, so students who are at-risk for drug use are most in need of activities during this time. Angell concludes the government should fund initiatives that are better at fighting teen drug abuse, such as counseling and after-school programs.

Angell writes policy materials for the organization Students for Sensible Drug Policy, an international network of students who oppose current drug policy, claiming it is counterproductive to the problem of drug abuse.

AS YOU READ, CONSIDER THE FOLLOWING QUESTIONS:
1. Who is Dr. Howard Taras and how does he factor into the author's argument?
2. What kinds of drugs does Angell say tested teens may be encouraged to use, and why?
3. What organizations oppose student drug testing, according to Angell?

President [George W.] Bush has requested $17.9 million in FY [fiscal year] 2008 to fund the Office of National Drug Control Policy [ONDCP] and Department of Education's [DOE] random suspicionless student drug testing grants program. While proponents of testing claim that it keeps teens away from drugs, research shows that the practice fails to reduce youth drug use and can actually make existing school drug problems worse. Drug testing students is also very expensive and invasive.

A 2003 study funded by the National Institute on Drug Abuse [NIDA]—the largest of its kind—examined 94,000 students at 900 schools in the U.S. and found no difference between levels of drug use at schools that test their students and those that do not. The study concluded, "[S]chool drug testing was not associated with either the prevalence or frequency of student marijuana use, or of other illicit drug use." Dr. Lloyd Johnston, one of the three University of Michigan researchers who conducted the study, commented, "[Drug testing is] the kind of intervention that doesn't win the hearts and minds of children. I don't think it brings about any constructive changes in their attitudes about drugs or their belief in the dangers associated with using them."

Testing Worsens the Problem

In addition to being ineffective, there is evidence suggesting drug testing actually exacerbates the problem of teen drug abuse. Because most schools that test do so as a condition of participating in

What Drugs Can Be Detected by a Student Drug Testing Program?

Drug tests can detect a wide number of substances, depending on whether an oral swab, a urine specimen, or a combination of urine and hair specimens is used. However, tests are not effective for all drugs, which some say encourages students to use the drugs that cannot be detected by tests.

Substance	Oral Swab	Urine	Urine and Hair
Amphetamines	●	●	●
Benzodiazepines (BZD)	●	●	
Barbiturates (BAR)	●	●	
Cocaine	●	●	●
Ecstasy (MDMA)		●	
Marijuana Tetrahydrocannabinol (THC)	●	●	●
Methadone (MTD)	●		
Methamphetamine (MET)	●	●	
Morphine			
Opiates (codeine, morphine, and heroin)	●	●	●
Oxycodone (OXY)			
Phencyclidine (PCP)	●	●	●
Propoxyphene (PPX)	●		
Tricyclic Antidepressant (TCA)			

Taken from: Student Drug-Testing Institute, "Developing, Implementing, and Sustaining a Student Drug-Testing Program," August 5, 2009, p. 16.

extra-curricular activities, at-risk students may be deterred from getting involved in such activities rather than from using drugs. Research shows that teen drug use and other dangerous behavior is highest between 3:00 and 6:00 P.M.—the unsupervised hours between the end of the school day and the time parents get home from work. As a result, those who choose not to submit to drug tests sacrifice extracurricular involvement and are at greater risk of abusing drugs or engaging in other dangerous behavior. According to Dr. Howard Taras, chair of the American Academy of Pediatrics Committee on School Health, "[Drug testing] may decrease involvement in extracurricular activities among students who regularly use or have once used drugs. Without engagement in healthy activities, adolescents are more likely to drop out of school, become pregnant, join gangs, pursue substance abuse and engage in other risky behaviors."

In addition, students may turn to more dangerous but less detectable drugs in order to avoid testing positive. Reasoning that marijuana is the most detectable drug, students may be driven to use other "harder" drugs, like meth, ecstasy, inhalants, or cocaine, which are far less detectable. False positives—when drug tests erroneously reveal drug use in students who have not used drugs—are relatively common, leading to the improper punishment of innocent students.

Invest in Counselors Instead of Tests

With costs ranging between $10 and $75 per test, it is unconscionable for federal dollars to be earmarked for a program of questionable effectiveness while schools struggle to adequately pay teachers and fund valuable extracurricular programs. One school in Dublin, Ohio, for example, canceled its $35,000 per year drug testing program after determining it was not cost-effective. Of 1,473 students tested at $24 each, 11 tested positive, for a total cost of $3,200 per "positive" student. After canceling the program, the school used the savings to hire a full-time counselor and provided prevention programs that reached all 3,581 students.

Many schools that drug test require students to produce urine samples while school officials stand outside the door listening for the sounds of urination to guard against tampered specimens. In addition to putting school officials at risk of being sued for sexual assault, this is invasive and embarrassing for students, and sends the message that they are guilty until proven innocent. Students need to know that they can go to school officials for help if they have problems with drugs, but random suspicionless testing poisons important relationships of trust between students and educators and makes it less likely that alienated adolescents will seek help when they need it.

In the event of positive test results, schools often ask students to provide lists of prescription and over-the-counter medications they are taking in order to ascertain whether or not those drugs may have produced a false positive. This means that students taking birth control or antidepressants may be forced to disclose this information to school officials.

Questionable Legality

According to the 2003 NIDA study, 95 percent of American schools do not randomly drug test their student athletes, and only two percent of schools randomly test students who participate in extracurriculars other than athletics. Prominent organizations that oppose random suspicionless student drug testing include the National Education Association, the Association for Addiction Professionals, the American Public Health Association, the American Academy of Pediatrics, the National Association of Social Workers, and the National Council on Alcoholism and Drug Dependence.

While the Supreme Court narrowly ruled (by a 5–4 margin) in 2002 that schools can require students involved in competitive extracurricular activities to submit to drug tests, it is important to note that the Court's ruling on the constitutionality of student drug testing only interpreted federal law. Many state laws and constitutions provide additional protections for student privacy. In fact, lawsuits have been filed against school districts in several states over their student drug testing policies. This means that schools electing to drug test their students are subject to tremendous legal liability. Laws vary greatly from state to state, and in the absence of state court decisions upholding drug testing, school districts run

Some schools have opted to cancel their drug testing programs in favor of counseling and prevention programs.

the serious risk of financial ruin in the event of a lawsuit, even when successfully defended. Even in cases where drug testing is legally permissible, the mere appearance of mishandling sensitive medical information or misconduct in administering the tests can invite litigation. This increases the actual cost of drug testing programs due to the need to hire attorneys to ensure legal compliance and to purchase tort insurance to protect against potential lawsuits

Fund Programs That Work

In 2006, ONDCP/DOE granted money to 66 school districts with 362 schools, each grant averaging approximately $125,000. The schools must include in the random testing pool all students who participate in athletic programs and/or all who are engaged in competitive extra-curricular school-sponsored activities.

There are many deserving programs that are under-funded, yet are actually effective at keeping teens healthy and out of trouble. Such programs that the president has suggested eliminating include the Mental Health Integration in Schools Program, the Elementary and Secondary School Counseling Program, Mentoring Programs, and the School Dropout Prevention Program.

EVALUATING THE AUTHOR'S ARGUMENTS:

Tom Angell quotes from several sources to support the points he makes in his viewpoint. Make a list of everyone he quotes, including their credentials and the nature of their comments. Then, analyze his sources—are they credible? Are they well qualified to speak on this subject? What specific points do they support?

Drug Testing Does Not Encourage Drug Use

Robert DuPont

"[Drug testing] programs offer students a good reason not to use drugs."

In the following viewpoint Robert DuPont argues that drug testing does not encourage drug use among tested students. He discusses a comprehensive 2010 study by the US Department of Education that found students who are tested for drug use during the school year have a lower rate of drug use than students who are not tested. DuPont says teen drug use can be lowered further by testing not only athletes or students who participate in extracurricular activities but also the entire student body. DuPont concludes that testing programs offer students an excuse to say no when peer pressured to try drugs, and evidence shows that schools with testing programs have fewer drug problems than schools without testing programs.

DuPont is president of the Institute for Behavior and Health, an organization that identifies and promotes strategies intended to reduce the demand for illegal drugs. DuPont also served as the first director of the National Institute on Drug Abuse, from 1973 to 1978.

AS YOU READ, CONSIDER THE FOLLOWING QUESTIONS:
1. What percentage of students subjected to mandatory random student drug testing test positive for substance use in the past thirty days, according to DuPont?
2. What percentage of students not subjected to mandatory random student drug testing test positive for substance use in the past thirty days, as cited by the author?
3. What does the phrase "spillover effect" mean in the context of the viewpoint?

A [2010] study released by the U.S. Department of Education Institute of Education Sciences conducted an experimental evaluation of mandatory random student drug testing (MRSDT) programs in 36 high schools within 7 school districts. About half of the schools in each district were randomly assigned to the treatment group and half to the control group. Treatment schools began implementing MRSDT programs while control schools did not.

MRSDT programs in public schools are limited to students who participate in athletics and extracurricular activities. In this study, some of the testing pools in schools with MRSDT were comprised of only athletes while others included athletes and extracurricular activity participants, leaving many students untested in those schools. The frequency of drug testing and drug test panels in schools with MRSDT programs varied. All seven school districts tested for marijuana, amphetamines, and methamphetamines. Cocaine and opiates were included in six of the seven district panels. Districts also tested for an assortment of other substances.

Students in all schools were surveyed and tracked over one year. Researchers compared students who participated in activities which made them subject to drug testing in schools with MRSDT to students who participated in the same activities in schools without MRSDT. Results are encouraging and provide extensive support of MRSDT programs.

Tested Students Use Drugs Less Often
Students subject to MRSDT reported a statistically significant lower rate of past 30-day use of substances included in their schools' drug

testing panels (16%) than comparable students in schools without MRSDT (22%). This included alcohol for three districts and nicotine for two districts. Similar differences were also found between the two groups on other substance use measures, though [these] were not statistically significant.

Contrary to what *USA Today* reports in "High school drug testing shows no long-term effect on use" (July 15, 2010), this study has demonstrated the value of MRSDT. Specifically *USA Today* highlights that MRSDT did not impact students' plans to use drugs in the future. It is true that there was no difference between the percentage of students subject to MRSDT (34%) and the percentage not subject to MRSDT (33%) that reported they planned to use substances within the next 12 months. However, MRSDT programs subject eligible students to random drug testing during the school year only; the summer months are a time when student substance use is no longer monitored. MRSDT programs are designed to deter substance use when students are in school. This study demonstrates that MRSDT is effective at achieving this goal.

> **FAST FACT**
>
> A study by the US Department of Education's Institute of Education Sciences showed that schools without mandatory random student drug testing had a higher incidence of students using drugs in the past month (22 percent) than did schools with mandatory student drug testing (16 percent).

Expanding Testing Programs

It is sometimes claimed that drug testing programs deter student participation in extracurricular activities. In this study, MRSDT had no effect on the participation rates by students in activities that subjected them to drug testing. Nearly the same percentage of students in schools with MRSDT participated in activities covered by their schools' testing programs (53%) as the percentage of students in schools without MRSDT who participated in such activities (54%). This indicates that students in schools with MRSDT programs knew their participation in such activities subjected them to testing and it did not deter them from participation.

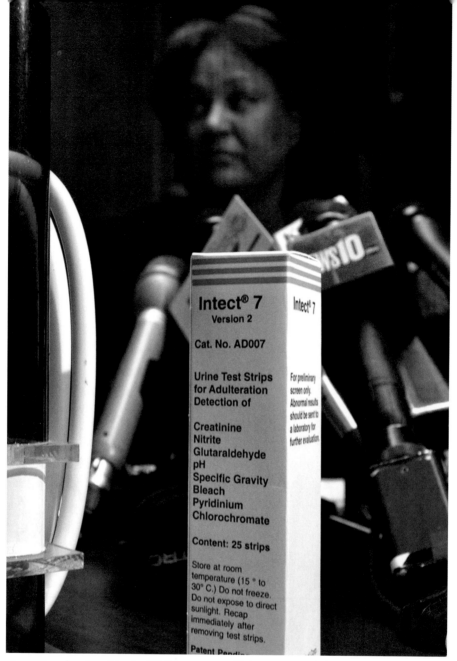

A 2010 study released by the US Department of Education revealed that mandatory random student drug testing programs are effective in decreasing substance abuse by students.

USA Today is critical of this study because there was no spillover effect on students who were not subject to MRSDT in schools with testing programs. This is not a surprise considering the MRSDT programs were studied for one year of implementation. As drug testing programs expand and include options for students to voluntarily enter the testing pool (as opposed to mandatory participation only through extracurricular activities), a spillover effect in time is possible.

A Reason to Say No

Random student drug testing programs reinforce schools' comprehensive substance use prevention programs as a deterrent against youth substance use. These programs offer students a good reason not to use drugs, including alcohol and tobacco which can be included in testing panels along with other illegal drugs. Voluntary random drug testing programs also are used in public schools either as a single option or in combination with a mandatory program. This allows students, with a parent's permission, to make an active choice to participate in random drug testing. The U.S. Department of Education is to be commended for supporting this ambitious study and shedding light on the many benefits of school-based random student drug testing programs.

EVALUATING THE AUTHOR'S ARGUMENTS:

To make his argument Robert DuPont cites a 2010 study by the US Department of Education. This is the same study that was discussed by Jacob Sullum in viewpoint 4 in this chapter, although Sullum came to very different conclusions about what the study means. Does it surprise you that DuPont and Sullum used the same evidence to arrive at such different conclusions? Why or why not? After reviewing both of their arguments, what is your opinion about the 2010 study—do you think it shows that student drug testing programs work, or not?

Facts About Student Drug Testing

The Drug & Alcohol Testing Industry Association (DATIA) has more than sixty member companies that are nationally accredited to administer drug and alcohol tests. These include companies based in states such as Texas, New Jersey, Florida, and California.

According to the National Institute on Drug Abuse (NIDA), drug tests can be run on all the following samples:
- urine
- hair
- saliva
- sweat

According to the University of Michigan:
- approximately 19 percent of American secondary schools have some type of student drug testing program;
- about 5 percent of the schools surveyed said they test athletes; and
- about 2 percent of the schools surveyed said they test students participating in other extracurricular activities.

The Alvin Independent School District in Texas tests students for any drug that is labeled illegal by the Food and Drug Administration or by the state of Texas. These include:
- alcohol
- amphetamines/methamphetamines
- anabolic steroids
- barbiturates
- benzodiazepines
- cocaine metabolites
- hallucinogens
- marijuana
- MDMA (Ecstasy)
- methadone
- nicotine

- opiates
- phencyclidine
- propoxyphene

As reported by MSNBC.com in 2009, only three states have statewide steroid testing:
- New Jersey
- Texas
- Illinois

Florida's statewide drug testing program was suspended due to budget constraints.

By 2008 twenty-nine states had received money from the US Department of Education's Office of Safe and Drug-Free Schools to develop or expand student drug testing programs.

Facts About the Effectiveness of Student Drug Testing Programs

According to the Student Drug-Testing Coalition:
- 94 percent of principals polled believe their school's random drug testing policy discourages drug and alcohol use among students;
- 73 percent of the principals reported a decrease in drug usage (compared with the period without a random drug testing program) among drug tested students;
- 25 percent of principals reported that drug use "remained the same";
- 2 percent of principals reported an increase in drug usage;
- 40 percent of principals reported that fewer students had been suspended from participation in athletic programs from drug use since reimplementation of the random drug testing program; and
- 86 percent of the high school principals surveyed stated that the random drug test is conducted using urinalysis.

According to a 2008 report by the Drug-Free Projects Coalition, Inc.:
- in New Jersey, the fifty-two schools with random student drug testing (RSDT) had a higher daily attendance than schools without RSDT (94.8 percent vs. 89.8 percent);

- students subject to RSDT scored higher, on average, on the SAT than students not subject to RSDT; and
- suspension and drop-out rates were lower at schools with RSDT.

Opinions About Student Drug Testing

According to a 2002 CNN/*USA Today*/Gallup poll that asked whether schools should be allowed to test students for illegal drugs before they can participate in nonathletic activities:

- 70 percent of adults responding said they thought student drug testing should be allowed;
- 29 percent responded that student drug testing should not be allowed; and
- 1 percent had no opinion.

Facts About the Legality of Student Drug Testing

Two US Supreme Court rulings have maintained that it is constitutional to perform random student drug testing on students involved in athletics and/or competitive extracurricular activities:

- *Vernonia School District 47J v. Acton,* 1995: 6 to 3 ruling that it was constitutional to require all athletes to take a urinalysis drug test in order to participate in athletics.
- *Board of Education of Independent School District No. 92 of Pottawatomie County, et al., Petitioners v. Lindsay Earls, et al.,* 2002: 5 to 4 ruling that it was constitutional to require all middle and high school students in Tecumseh, Oklahoma, to take a urinalysis drug test in order to participate in any extracurricular activities.

The United States Court of Appeals likewise ruled in two separate cases that student drug testing is legal when students have parking passes for school property or when they are driving on school property.

- *Todd, et al. v. Rush County Schools* (1998)
- *Joy v. Penn-Harris-Madison School Corp.* (2002)

In the 2008 case *York v. Wahkiakum,* Washington State's supreme court banned student drug testing on the basis that it violates the state constitution's position on privacy rights.

Facts About Student Drug Use

According to the *2009 National Survey on Drug Use and Health* conducted by the Substance Abuse and Mental Health Services Administration (SAMHSA):

- among youths aged twelve to seventeen, the current illicit drug use rate increased from 2008 (9.3 percent) to 2009 (10.0 percent);
- marijuana was the most commonly used illicit drug, and among persons aged twelve or older, the rate of past-month marijuana use was 6.6 percent, and the number of users was 16.7 million; and
- 10.0 percent of youths aged twelve to seventeen were current illicit drug users:
    - 7.3 percent used marijuana,
    - 3.1 percent engaged in nonmedical use of prescription psychotherapeutics,
    - 1.0 percent used inhalants,
    - 0.9 percent used hallucinogens, and
    - 0.3 percent used cocaine.

According to the PRIDE Survey's *National Summary 2009–2010, Grades 6–12:*

- approximately 21 percent of students report using illicit drugs of some kind;
- more than 14 percent of students report that they first used illicit drugs of some kind by the age of twelve; and
- males in the twelfth grade report using heroin almost three times as often as females in the twelfth grade report using heroin.

Facts About Students' Perception of the Availability of Drugs

According to the *2009 National Survey on Drug Use and Health* conducted by SAMHSA:

- almost half (49.9 percent) of youths aged twelve to seventeen reported in 2009 that it would be "fairly easy" or "very easy" for them to obtain marijuana;
- approximately one in five reported it would be easy to get cocaine (20.9 percent);

- about one in seven (13.5 percent) indicated that LSD would be "fairly" or "very" easily available; and
- one in eight (12.9 percent) indicated that heroin would be "fairly" or "very" easily available.

According to *Monitoring the Future: National Results on Adolescent Drug Use 2010 Overview* conducted by NIDA:
- 41 percent of eighth graders, 69 percent of tenth graders, and 82 percent of twelfth graders reported its being "fairly" or "very" easy to get marijuana;
- 36 percent of twelfth graders said it was "fairly" or "very" easy to get cocaine;
- approximately 20 percent of twelfth graders said it was "fairly" or "very" easy to get heroin;
- approximately 30 percent of tenth graders said it was "fairly" or "very" easy to get narcotics such as Oxycontin;
- approximately 38 percent of twelfth graders said it was "fairly" or "very" easy to get Ecstasy; and
- fewer than 30 percent of eighth, tenth, and twelfth graders consider steroids "fairly" or "very" easy to get, despite no longer being allowed to be sold over the counter.

Organizations to Contact

The editors have compiled the following list of organizations concerned with the issues debated in this book. The descriptions are derived from materials provided by the organizations. All have publications or information available for interested readers. The list was compiled on the date of publication of the present volume; the information provided here may change. Be aware that many organizations take several weeks or longer to respond to inquiries, so allow as much time as possible for the receipt of requested materials.

American Civil Liberties Union (ACLU)
125 Broad St., 18th Fl., New York, NY 10004
(212) 549-2500
website: www.aclu.org

Founded in the early twentieth century, the ACLU's goal has always been to protect and defend the civil liberties of citizens as defined by the US Constitution. These liberties include freedom of speech, freedom of religion, due process, and the right to privacy. The organization boasts more than half a million members, including hundreds of attorneys and thousands of volunteers. The ACLU opposes mandatory student drug testing on the grounds that it violates student privacy.

American Council for Drug Education (ACDE)
50 Jay St., Brooklyn, NY 11201
(718) 222-6641
e-mail: acde@phoenixhouse.org
website: www.acde.org

The goal of the ACDE is to provide current and effective research to educate the population on drug use and prevention. Its programs and services are available to everyone from employers and educators to students and health care professionals. At the ACDE website, students will find a quiz on drug knowledge, as well as facts about drugs and their effects on the body.

The Center for Health and Health Care in Schools (CHHCS)
The George Washington University
2121 K St. NW, Ste. 250, Washington, DC 20037
(202) 466-3396 • fax (202) 466-3467
e-mail: chhcs@gwu.edu
website: www.healthinschools.org

Located at the George Washington University School of Public Health, this organization aims to improve the well-being of students across the country by developing health programs in schools. Working closely with educators, school administrators, and health care professionals, the CHHCS strives to ensure that children achieve healthier lives. Its award-winning website offers information for health care professionals, educators, and individuals on a variety of topics related to student drug testing and drug abuse.

Community Anti-Drug Coalitions of America (CADCA)
625 Slaters Ln., Ste. 300, Alexandria, VA 22314
(800) 54-CADCA • fax: (703) 706-0565
website: www.cadca.org

CADCA's mission is to help community coalitions create and maintain safe, healthy, and drug-free communities. It was founded in 1992 when organizers began training antidrug coalitions to identify and address drug abuse issues. Now more than five thousand antidrug coalitions can be found throughout the United States. CADCA's website includes information on training and events, as well as interactive media including blogs, photos, and video.

Drug & Alcohol Testing Industry Association (DATIA)
1325 G St. NW, Ste. 500 #5001, Washington, DC 20005
(800) 355-1257 • fax: (202) 315-3579
website: www.datia.org

Originally founded in 1995 as the National Association of Collection Sites, DATIA has more than a thousand members and aims to represent everyone in the drug testing industry, from collection sites to testing equipment manufacturers. Though one of its goals is to promote standards for the drug testing industry, another is to expand the drug testing market. Students can find the latest news on the site regarding drug testing and other drug issues.

Drug Free America Foundation, Inc. (DFAF)
5999 Central Ave., Ste. 301, Saint Petersburg, FL 33710
(727) 828-0211 • fax: (727) 828-0212
website: www.dfaf.org

One of the many objectives this United Nations–affiliated organization has is encouraging people to strive for drug-free homes, schools, workplaces, and communities. The DFAF focuses on policies and laws that will minimize illegal drug use and drug-related crime. A section of its website is for students and allows them to connect on social networking sites such as Facebook and Twitter.

Drug Policy Alliance (DPA)
70 W. Thirty-Sixth St., 16th Fl., New York, NY 10018
(212) 613-8020 • fax: (212) 613-8021
e-mail: nyc@drugpolicy.org
website: www.drugpolicy.org

One of the DPA's major aims is to educate readers about alternatives in the war against drugs, which it believes to be more detrimental than helpful. The alliance cites the use of science, compassion, health, and human rights as instrumental to its success. One of the organization's recent accomplishments includes a program in New Mexico to educate teenagers about issues related to methamphetamine use.

Institute for Behavior and Health, Inc. (IBH)
6191 Executive Blvd., Rockville, MD 20850
(301) 231-9010 • fax: (301) 770-6876
e-mail: contactus@ibhinc.org
website: www.ibhinc.org

Established in 1978, the IBH is a nonpartisan and nongovernmental organization whose goal is to minimize the demand for illicit drugs. The institute works with other organizations and groups to achieve this goal through various programs and policies. Its website has an extensive list of links to other organizations and programs.

National School Boards Association (NSBA)
1680 Duke St., Alexandria, VA 22314
(703) 838-6722 • fax: (703) 683-7590

e-mail: info@nsba.org
website: www.nsba.org

The NSBA, founded in 1940, works with school boards to advocate for fairness and excellence in public education. The association oversees more than 50 million public school students in the United States. Though it is headquartered in Washington, DC, this nonprofit organization establishes policies and services nationwide. The NSBA supports student drug testing and offers a plethora of reports and other documents on its site.

Save Our Society From Drugs (S.O.S.)

5999 Central Ave., Ste. 301, St. Petersburg, FL 33710
e-mail: info@saveoursociety.org
website: www.saveoursociety.org

This nonprofit organization focuses on the creation and promotion of drug laws in order to prevent illegal drug use. Another important focus of S.O.S. is to educate both the general population and lawmakers in particular about the negative effects of drugs on individuals and society. The organization is opposed to medical marijuana use and in favor of random student drug testing.

Students for Sensible Drug Policy (SSDP)

1623 Connecticut Ave. NW, Ste. 300, Washington, DC 20009
(202) 293-4414 • fax: (202) 293-8344
e-mail: ssdp@ssdp.org
website: www.ssdp.org

Unlike many other drug policy organizations, the SSDP is built around a network of students who in turn encourage other students to become active in the political process related to drug policy. In particular, they seek to change policies that are most detrimental to students. This is a grassroots organization that encourages students around the country to start their own local chapter of SSDP, thus learning the important issues surrounding activism.

US Department of Education

Office of Safe and Drug-Free Schools (OSDFS)
550 Twelfth St. SW, 10th Fl., Washington, DC 20202
(202) 245-7896 • fax: (202) 485-0013

e-mail: osdfs.safeschl@ed.gov
website: www.ed.gov/about/offices/list/osdfs

This government agency strives to bring drug education and assistance with creating drug-free policies to schools and universities across the United States. OSDFS strongly emphasizes drug prevention, both at the state and national levels. Its website provides information about national and state programs, reports, and news related to creating safe and drug-free schools.

US Drug Enforcement Administration (DEA)
8701 Morrissette Dr., Springfield, VA 22152
(202) 307-1000
website: www.justice.dea.gov

Created by President Richard Nixon in 1973, the DEA was created for the purpose of waging a war on the problem of drug abuse. More than three decades later, the DEA employs more than five thousand agents and has outposts in more than sixty countries around the world. Its mission remains to enforce laws related to controlled substances. The DEA aims to bring to justice people who grow, manufacture, or distribute illegal drugs. Its website includes information for young adults about drug prevention.

White House Office of National Drug Control Policy (ONDCP)
PO Box 6000, Rockville, MD 20849-6000
(800) 666-3332 • fax: (301) 519-5212
website: www.whitehousedrugpolicy.gov

The ONDCP, established by President Ronald Reagan in 1988, seeks to minimize illegal drug manufacturing, drug abuse, and the consequent crime and health problems caused by both. Its website includes comprehensive information about various drug types and on student drug testing programs around the nation.

For Further Reading

Books

Anonymous. *Go Ask Alice.* New York: Simon Pulse, 2005. This novel, which was first published more than a quarter of a century ago, is written in a memoir style, chronicling the author's descent into drug use.

Conyers, Beverly. *Addict in the Family: Stories of Loss, Hope, and Recovery.* Center City, MN: Hazelden Foundation, 2003. This compilation, written by the mother of a heroin addict, seeks to provide information about dealing with addiction and recovery.

Finley, Laura, and Peter S. Finley. *Piss Off! How Drug Testing and Other Privacy Violations Are Alienating America's Youth.* Monroe, ME: Common Courage Press, 2005. This book examines the legal precedents and social norms that inform current school policies, suggesting that intrusive policies yield negative results.

Gahlinger, Paul. *Illegal Drugs: A Complete Guide to their History, Chemistry, Use, and Abuse.* New York: Plume, 2004. This book begins with the discovery and early history of drugs and then thoroughly covers the war on drugs and current issues regarding drug abuse in the United States.

Kuhn, Cynthia, Scott Swartzwelder, and Wilkie Wilson. *Buzzed: The Straight Facts About the Most Used and Abused Drugs from Alcohol to Ecstasy.* 3rd ed. New York: Norton, 2008. Covering several kinds of drugs ranging from caffeine to alcohol to heroin, this book aims to educate readers about different drugs. A glossary of drug terminology is included in the book.

Radev, Anna, ed. *I've Got This Friend Who: Advice for Teens and Their Friends on Alcohol, Drugs, Eating Disorders, Risky Behavior and More.* Center City, MN: Hazelden Foundation, 2007. Written by experts at the nonprofit organization KidsPeace, this book attempts to give teens honest answers and advice regarding behaviors and issues that affect their lives.

Periodicals and Internet Sources

Express Times (Lehigh Valley, PA). "Opinion: Expand Random Drug Testing in Schools," October 5, 2010. www.lehighvalleylive.com /today/index.ssf/2010/10/opinion_expand_random_drug_tes.html.

Grau, Hal. "Should High School Athletes Be Tested for Steroids?," *Frederick (MD) News Post*, August 29, 2010. www.fredericknews post.com/sections/sports/display.htm?storyid=109177.

Grunwell, Rachel. "Drug Tests Spark School Probe," *New Zealand Herald* (Auckland), February 7, 2010. www.nzherald.co.nz/nz /news/article.cfm?c_id=1&objectid=10624642.

Houston Chronicle. "Side Effects: Test Student Athletes in Texas for Steroids, but Do It Wisely," December 6, 2007. www.chron.com /disp/story.mpl/editorial/5359056.html.

Kocieniewski, David. "Is This the Answer to Drug Use?," *New York Times*, March 25, 2007. www.nytimes.com/2007/03/25/nyregion /nyregionspecial2/25RDRUG.html?_r=1.

Landauer, Michael. "Steroid Testing Has Always Been About Sending a Message," *Dallas Morning News*, August 21, 2009. http://dal lasmorningviewsblog.dallasnews.com/archives/2009/08/post-49 .html.

Lyon, Lindsay. "7 Reasons Parents Should Not Test Kids for Drug Use," *U.S. News & World Report*, August 6, 2008. http://health .usnews.com/health-news/articles/2008/08/06/7-reasons-parents -should-not-test-kids-for-drug-use.html?PageNr=l.

Mohl, Evan. "Steroid Testing Not Worth the Money," *Daily News* (Galveston County, TX), March 26, 2010. http://galvestondaily news.com/story.lasso?ewcd=a0086fff529ce737.

O'Hagan, Maureen. "WA High Court Says Random School Drug Testing Unconstitutional," *Seattle Times*, March 13, 2008. http:// seattletimes.nwsource.com/html/localnews/2004279865_web drugtests13m.html.

Pensacola (FL) News Journal. "Viewpoint: Drug Test Policy Is Wasteful, Ineffective," February 7, 2011. www.pnj.com/arti cle/20110207/OPINION/102070302/Viewpoint-Drug-test -policy-is-wasteful-ineffective.

Roan, Shari. "Put to the Test," *Los Angeles Times*, May 21, 2007. www.latimes.com/features/health/la-he-drugtesting21may21,1,4 356795,full.story?coll=la-headlines-health.

Roanoke (VA) Times. "Drug Testing in Schools," August 16, 2010. www.roanoke.com/editorials/wb/257058.

Rosenbaum, Marsha. "No Quick Fix," *USA Today*, May 7, 2007. www.usatoday.com/news/opinion/2007-05-07-oppose_n.htm.

San Diego Union-Tribune. "Random Drug Testing at Southern Nevada High School Working," February 10, 2008. http://legacy .signonsandiego.com/news/education/20080210-1259-nv-drug testing.html.

Star (Toronto). "Why Not Randomly Drug Test High School Athletes?," June 15, 2010. http://thestar.blogs.com/school sports/2010/06/why-not-randomnly-drug-test-high-school-ath letes.html.

Sullivan, Andy. "More Drug Tests in Schools Urged by White House: Some Parents Cite Student Privacy Violations," *Boston Globe*, March 20, 2006. www.boston.com/news/nation/washing ton/articles/2006/03/20/more_drug_tests_in_schools_urged_by _white_house.

Sun Sentinel (South Florida). "Drug Testing Student Athletes Shows Promise at Key Time," January 6, 2011. http://articles .sun-sentinel.com/2011-01-06/news/fl-editorial-drug-tests -nb-0106-20110106_1_drug-testing-student-athletes-teen-drug -illegal-drugs.

Tynan, Matthew. "Many Student Athletes React Favorably to Drug Testing in City Schools," *Juneau (AK) Empire*, September 29, 2009. www.juneauempire.com/stories/092009/loc_495158483.shtml.

Vumbaca, Gino. "Drug Tests Make No Sense," *Age* (Australia), March 27, 2008. www.theage.com.au/news/opinion/drug-tests-make-no -sense/2008/03/26/1206207203904.html?page=fullpage#content Swap1.

Websites

Just Think Twice (www.justthinktwice.com). This site, associated with the US Drug Enforcement Administration, aims to educate young people about the facts and consequences of drug use and abuse. A special "Teens Ask Teens" section allows readers to ask questions about issues related to drug use, including drug testing at schools.

National Institute on Drug Abuse for Teens (NIDA for Teens) (www.teens.drugabuse.gov). As an organization, NIDA has two main goals: to support research about drug abuse issues and to make the results of that research available to the public. One of the ways NIDA disseminates information to teens is through this website. The blog addresses issues such as drug testing and presents research regarding this issue.

The Partnership at Drugfree.org (www.drugfree.org). Formerly known as the Partnership for a Drug-Free America, this organization's website is an advertising method to "unsell" drugs to young people. Resources on the site include a drug guide, a newsletter, blogs, and even videos from involved celebrities such as actress Melissa Gilbert.

Prevention Not Punishment (www.preventionnotpunishment.org). Created by the nonpartisan and nongovernmental organization called the Institute for Behavior and Health (IBH), this website promotes random student drug testing. It serves as an informative resource for parents, students, and school administrators to learn more about the facts and effects of random student drug testing.

Safety First Project (www.drugtestingfails.org). This website, established by the Drug Policy Alliance, offers publications and information for parents, educators, and students about the realities of drugs and drug abuse. A thrust of the site's message is the opposition to random student drug testing programs. Students can access its publication "Making Sense of Student Drug Testing: Why Educators Are Saying No" online.

Stop the Drug War (http://stopthedrugwar.org). This site, hosted by DRCNet, focuses more on the legalization of drugs rather than on ways to prevent drug abuse. Its coverage on the drug war is aimed not at drug testing but at supporting stricter drug regulation and control.

The Student Drug-Testing Coalition (www.studentdrugtesting .org). This comprehensive website provides information on drug use, drug legislation, drug testing methods, and schools that enforce student drug testing. The site maintains that nonpunitive drug testing is an effective deterrent to drug abuse.

Index

T

Tallassee City Schools (AL), experience of mandatory drug testing program in, 89–93

Taras, Howard, 20, 103

Taylor's Law (TX), 48, 51

Todd et al. v. Rush County Schools (1998), 24

Tulia Independent School District, Bean v. (2003), 79

U

University of Texas University Interscholastic League, 8, 58

USA Today (newspaper), 109, 110

V

Vernonia School District 47J v. Acton (1995), 40, 41, *44*

Vicodin, 40

W

Wahkiakum, York v. (WA, 2008), 35

Walters, John, 17, *17*

Y

York v. Wahkiakum (WA, 2008), 35

Picture Credits

© AP Images/Harry Cabluck, 59

© AP Images/Damian Dovarganes, 49

© AP Images/Mike Fuentes, 53

© AP Images/Javier Galeano, 17

© AP Images/Rich Pedroncelli, 110

© AP Images/Sang Tam, 10, 96

© AP Images/The Shawnee News-Star, Kim Morava, 42

© AP Images/Evan Vucci, 92

© AP Images/Ronen Zilberman, 46

© Bill Bachmann/Alamy, 78

© BSIP/Photo Researchers, Inc., 30

© Bubbles Photolibrary/Alamy, 14

© Ted Foxx/Alamy, 34

Gale/Cengage Learning, 13, 19, 25, 36, 44, 50, 55, 65, 87, 98, 102

© Dennis MacDonald/Alamy, 68

© Cordelia Molloy/Photo Researchers, Inc., 23

© RIA Novosti/Photo Researchers, Inc., 75

© Blair Seitz/Photo Researchers, Inc., 105